GOLDEN

Old & New

a walking tour guide *by* **Cathleen Norman**

This project was partially funded by a State Historical Fund grant award from the Colorado Historical Society, with additional funding from the Golden Civic Foundation, the Golden Urban Renewal Authority, and the City of Golden. The project was carried out with the assistance of the Golden Planning Department and the 1996 Golden Historic Preservation Board.

Cover photo by Susan Goldstein

International Standard Book Number: 0-9654343-0-3
Text copyright @ 1996 City of Golden
Photographs copyright @ 1996 Susan Goldstein where noted

Published by
Preservation Publishing
459 South Routt Way
Lakewood, Colorado 80226

Printed in Colorado by Mountain West Printing Ltd.

Credits

Cathleen Norman, writer and editor
Susan Goldstein, photographer
Dan Abbott, historical consultant
Nancy Lund, cover design

Table of Contents

Golden Old and New 1

Golden Beginnings 2

Map of Golden 6

Tour 1 - Twelfth Street Neighborhood 8

Tour 2 - Washington Avenue 20

Tour 3 - Courthouse Hill/School of Mines Campus 34

Tour 4 - North Side Neighborhood 50

Tour 5 - East Golden Neighborhood 62

Other Sites 77

Preserving Golden's Architecture: How It Works 78

Glossary 79

Bibliography 83

This early photograph of Washington Avenue shows wooden false-fronted stores with majestic Castle Rock in the background.

Golden Old and New

The buildings of Golden tell its rich story. This guide takes you on five different tours that point out the city's most important buildings and homes, special because of their history and their architecture. While Golden is one of Colorado's oldest communities, it is also a mingling of old and new. As you walk through Golden, notice the historic buildings and homes that have been carefully preserved, and notice those that have been changed to meet modern needs.

Ask yourself: how does the new blend with the old? Is it harmonious? Are the additions or changes compatible with the original building? How do they influence the quality of the historic neighborhood?

Photo by Susan Goldstein

Twelfth Street Neighborhood

Golden Old and New contains five walking tours highlighting Golden's architectural heritage. Each walking tour is 1 to 2 miles long. Each tour lasts 1 to 2 hours, depending upon your walking speed and whether you explore optional sites. At the end of this book there is a list of museums and other places that you can visit individually.

This book also contains a glossary and a description of the historic preservation process in Golden, for those who want to find out more about how this historic city maintains its history.

Golden Beginnings

Golden was founded during the gold rush of 1859, but gold seekers were not its first inhabitants. The area had been frequented by the Ute, Arapaho, and Cheyenne tribes, as well as early trappers Louis Vasquez and Rufus Sage. Most sources agree that the town was named for settler Tom Golden, one of the early gulch miners who panned gold in the valley of Clear Creek.

A toll bridge, two stores, and the county's first commercial garden were among the settlers' first endeavors. Golden's location at the mouth of Clear Creek canyon furthered the town's aspirations as a supply center and aided its role as a transportation hub for freight wagons and, later, the railroad. "Our city is now full of energetic, go-ahead men enroute to the gold mines," reported the *Golden Mountaineer* in 1860.

Photo courtesy of Golden Pioneer Museum

This early view of Golden, prior to 1879, shows that the city was a scattering of buildings east of the mouth Clear Creek canyon.

Although Golden was site of the Territorial Capital from 1862 to 1867, it lost the state capital to Denver when Colorado achieved statehood. Instead, the town grew slowly but steadily as a supply center for the mining districts in the mountains to the west. Golden also grew as an industrial town. Clear Creek provided water for milling, smelting, manufacturing, and generating electricity. Local coal mines yielded resources for early industry and employed many local residents. Early Golden industries also included a cigar factory, candy factory, paper mill, glass plant, three lime kilns, and several stone quarries.

Town building was aided by the clay deposits that supplied material for local brickmaking. Wood was used less frequently in construction because it had to be brought down from Clear Creek canyon. However, cannonball-sized stones from the creek were used in foundations, retaining walls, and porches of many local buildings, as well as in the Armory Building at Thirteenth and Arapahoe (**#16** on **Tour 2**).

Agriculture was a chief Golden industry, made possible by irrigation from Clear Creek. The crops planted by David K. Wall in 1859 became the county's first commercial garden, and by 1902 the town was "surrounded on all sides by farming and stockraising," according to *Illustrated Golden*. Wheat was a major crop and accounted for the three flour mills. At one time, the Rock Flour Mill produced 200 barrels of flour a day. Orchards and vineyards grew on North Table Mountain, while Clear Creek Valley was filled with fruit trees and fields of strawberries and raspberries, as well as vegetable gardens. Farmers from east Golden came to town selling produce from their horse-drawn wagons.

Toll roads were Golden's first means of transportation; several routes were built to the mining districts. In 1870 the railroad arrived in Golden. The Colorado Central Railroad (later the Colorado & Southern) was headquartered here and served Idaho Springs, Georgetown, Central City, and Black Hawk. The railroad hauled sup-

*Railroads were key to Golden's early growth, shown in this picture from **The Colorado Miner**, January 1881.*

plies to the mining districts and returned with ore to be processed by local smelters. In the 1890s, interurban rail lines also brought visitors from Denver. During the mid-1900s, Golden became the hub of two transcontinental highways, Interstate 40 and Interstate 70, which helped promote the town as a tourist destination.

The first Jefferson County Courthouse

Although Golden lost the capital to Denver, it remained the Jefferson County seat and built a splendid brick courthouse that shared the hill with the Colorado School of Mines campus. This Victorian beauty was replaced in the 1960s by a boxy beige-brick building with an adjacent five-story Hall of Justice. In 1990, Jefferson County began construction on a new courthouse — the gleaming building that dominates the ridge southeast of town, gazing down at the state capitol on the plains below.

Golden became the site of the Colorado School of Mines in the 1870s. After a church-financed schoolhouse on the eastern edge of Golden blew down in a windstorm, a brick classroom was constructed on the present-day campus. City fathers W. A. H. Loveland, Charles C. Welch, and Edward L. Berthoud helped establish the college, either by serving on the board of trustees or by contributing funds or land to the fledgling school. Today the world-class institution offers degree programs that include engineering, geology, and environmental sciences.

By the early 1900s, Golden had grown into a proud city. The original county courthouse and the Colorado School of Mines are the focal point of this photo.

The Coors brewery is another early enterprise that has had a lasting influence in Golden. Founded by German immigrant Adolph Coors, the brewing company has grown from a small stone building near the foot of Castle Rock to an industrial complex that expands eastward along the Clear Creek Valley. Brewery tours have become a major attraction for visitors coming to Golden. In the early 1900s, Coors branched out into ceramics manufacturing, a sideline that later helped sustain the company during Prohibition. Today, Coors is the largest single-source brewery in the world, producing over twenty million barrels of beer per year.

THE GOLDEN BREWERY.
GOLDEN, COLORADO.

Coors Brewery began as a small stone building near Clear Creek in the 1870s.

Golden begins its second century poised as one of Jefferson County's leading communities. Diversified local industry, the new courthouse that graces the ridge south of town, a thriving downtown, and the recently-completed Visitors Center represent the city's optimistic outlook for the future. Golden struggles with the challenge of retaining its small town identity in the face of Denver's metropolitan suburbs expanding ever westward. However, the diligent efforts of the historic preservation board and dedicated local preservationists are ensuring that Golden's heritage lives on for future generations to enjoy.

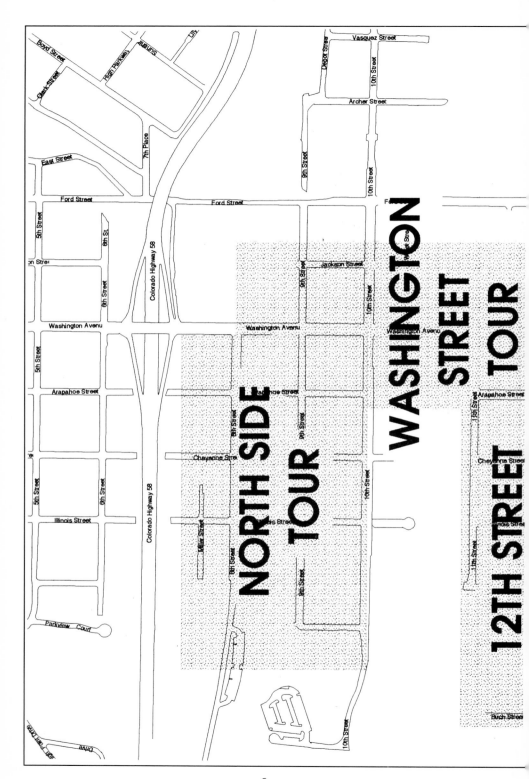

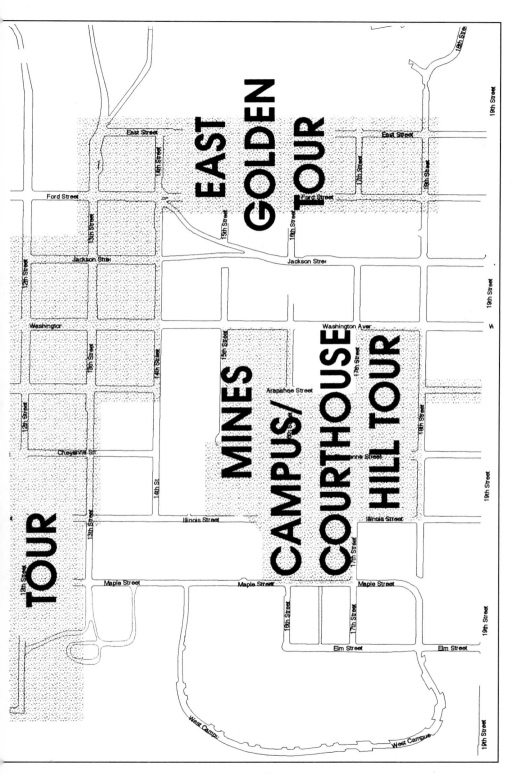

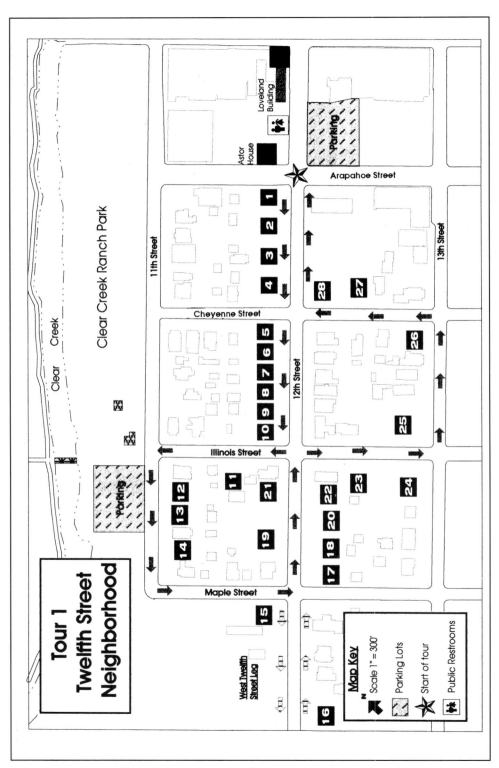

Tour 1
Twelfth Street
Neighborhood

Clear Creek Ranch Park

Clear Creek

Astor House

Loveland Building

Parking

Arapahoe Street

11th Street

Cheyenne Street

12th Street

13th Street

Illinois Street

Parking

Maple Street

West Twelfth Street Leg

Map Key

Scale 1" = 300'

Parking Lots

Start of tour

Public Restrooms

- 8 -

The Sorenson house at 1010 Twelfth Street, #7 on this tour.

Photo by Cathleen Norman

Tour 1

Twelfth Street Neighborhood

NR = National Register
LR = Local Register

1	900 Twelfth
2	906 Twelfth, **NR**
3	910 - 912 Twelfth
4	920 Twelfth
5	1000 Twelfth
6	1006 Twelfth, **LR**
7	1010 Twelfth
8	1014 Twelfth
9	1018 Twelfth, **LR**
10	1022 Twelfth
11	1114 Illinois
12	1107 Eleventh, **LR**
13	1109 Eleventh
14	1119 Eleventh
15	1112 - 1200 Twelfth
16	West End of Twelfth Street (optional)
17	1123 Twelfth, **LR**
18	1119 Twelfth
19	1114 Twelfth, **LR**
20	1111 Twelfth
21	1106 Twelfth, **LR**
22	1105 Twelfth
23	1210 Illinois
24	1100 Thirteenth
25	1221 Illinois
26	1220 Cheyenne
27	1221 Cheyenne
28	1205 Cheyenne

Tour 1 Twelfth Street Neighborhood
TIME 1 hour   DISTANCE 1.5 miles

TIPS   Cool and shady. Level streets. Public restrooms on Twelfth St. across from parking. Picnic tables at Clear Creek Ranch Park on Eleventh St.

This tour visits the Twelfth Street Historic Residential District, listed in the National Register of Historic Places. These quiet shady streets are where Golden's early civic leaders and merchants made their homes. Business managers, dentists, doctors, and druggists also lived here, within walking distance of their stores and offices. School of Mines professors too resided in this neighborhood, and Mines students rented rooms in some of the larger houses. Residents also included workers at the west Twelfth Street industrial sites, such as the White Ash coal mine, the now-demolished Colorado School of Mines Experimental Plant, and the Parfet/Rubey clay pits.

The neighborhood reflects the simple tastes of Golden's early residents. Graceful, gabled homes were built in plain and unpretentious styles of the 1870s and 1880s, styles seen in other territorial towns like Idaho Springs, Georgetown, Central City, and Denver's oldest neighborhoods. Brick was predominantly used, taking advantage of the abundant local clay deposits and local brickyards. Some homes were adorned with decorative shingles, bay windows, or wrap-around porches. A Local Landmark plaque identifies Golden homes and buildings with distinctive histories.

Photo by Susan Goldstein

A blend of old and new, the historic house at 1112 Twelfth Street is joined to a row of contemporary townhouses.

This gabled brick dwelling was the home of Joseph Standley, an early resident for whom a lake in Arvada was named. From 1888 to 1914 this was the residence of M. I. Morrill, manager of the Golden Illuminating Company, the local electric company. Extensive remodeling in the late 1920s removed the second story, stuccoed the brick, and enclosed the front porch — alterations that lend an English flavor. This home provides a picturesque entrance to the historic district, especially in summer when the garden is in bloom.

900 Twelfth St. **1**
Standley Residence
(1873)

Thomas Gow paid $700 to have this home built, and the Gow family lived here for two generations. The square bay window seen on other local houses of the 1870s and the decorative gable end give this Victorian cottage a romantic air.

906 Twelfth St. **2**
Gow Residence
(1879)
NR

The brick construction, recessed first story, corbeled brick cornice, and scrolled cutout design above the windows help this modern two-story building mingle with its historic neighbors.

910 - 912 Twelfth St. **3**
Earth Science Building
(1980s)

This splendid residence was the home of Dr. James Kelly, Golden's leading physician. Dr. Kelly practiced in an office in his home, ran a local drugstore, and was conveniently the town coroner. He was also mayor of Golden in 1880.

920 Twelfth St. **4**
Kelly Mansion
(1879)

This dwelling is Golden's fanciest Italianate residence, a style popular nationwide from the 1850s to the 1870s. The low-pitched roof, massive carved roof brackets, and tall thin windows are hallmarks of this style. Notice the returning gable ends. The beige-brick porch was added in 1903. The 3,392-square-foot house was subdivided into apartments in the mid-1900s; it has since been returned to a single residence. The Golden City Brewery operates out of the historic brick building behind the house and offer tours upon request.

5 **1000 Twelfth St.**
Collum House
(1902)

This two-story brick duplex has leaf and trefoil carvings above the windows, an embellishment seen on other Twelfth Street homes. Original owner John Collum was superintendent of the Malachite Smelter. The Malachite was one of a half-dozen smelters that operated on the banks of Clear Creek in the late 1800s, making use of Golden's ample supply of coal and water to process silver and gold ore from the Clear Creek mining districts.

Photo by Susan Goldstein

6 **1006 Twelfth St.**
Maddox Residence
(1903), **LR**

The prominent shingled roof and curved, turret-style dormer windows distinguish this Edwardian Vernacular style home. It was built for Reverend Maddox at a cost of $2,800. Wood-shingled dormers peer from the second story in the front and on both sides.

Later residents were Franklin and Laura Hills; Franklin was a chemist at the now-demolished Colorado School of Mines Research Institute at the west end of Twelfth St.

Photo by Susan Goldstein

7 **1010 Twelfth St.**
Sorenson Residence
(1897)

This graceful home is Edwardian Vernacular, a post-Victorian style that resembles the Queen Anne style but with fewer decorative details. This home has a curving wrap-around porch and gable-end shingles. Its original owner, Soren Sorenson, ran a grocery store on Washington Avenue in the early 1900s. Dr. Leslie C. Anderson built the two-story addition after 1947 to contain his dentist office. This attractive house has a shingle-clad "twin" at 922 19th Street.

Simon Parshall's Edwardian Vernacular home was built in 1893, the year of the Silver Panic. While bankruptcies and business failures jolted the state and the country, Golden's dependence on local clay and coal mining helped the town withstand this economic calamity. Like many local residents, Parshall worked for the railroad. He was a fireman and engineer for the Colorado Central Railroad which had headquarters in Golden. Upon quitting the railroad, he joined E. E. Stewart in running the grocery store at 922 Washington. The house resembles its neighbor to the east, with a wide front porch instead of a wrap-around.

1014 Twelfth St.
Parshall Residence
(1893)

8

This story-and-a-half brick home has steep Gothic Revival-style gables with spindlework and a knob-like finial. Its long thin windows are Italianate. The incongruous Colonial Revival door enclosure was added in the 1940s.

1018 Twelfth St.
West Residence
(1872), **LR**

9

Its owner, George West, was an original town founder, building the Boston Building, where he ran a printing press upstairs. West later published the *Colorado Transcript*, Colorado's oldest weekly newspaper. He lived here from 1873 to 1902, then moved to 1210 Illinois (**#23** on this tour). Golden High School principal Samuel Shipman later lived in this house.

Photo by Susan Goldstein

Owned by Ella Felt, this brick foursquare was built in a style popular throughout Colorado. The brick is an unusual salmon color. The two-story massing, hipped roof, wide roof overhangs, and the full front porch are typical foursquare elements.

1022 Twelfth St.
Felt Residence
(1903)

10

Built of clapboard siding, this home has a wide front porch and a shingled gable end. Originally a stable for the home at 1100 Twelfth Street, it was later expanded into a six-room dwelling at a cost of $1,000. It is now a three-bedroom house.

1114 Illinois St.
Knowles/Titus
Residence
(1904)

11

This early picture shows historic Clear Creek, wide enough to pose a serious threat of flooding to the people who lived on Eleventh Street.

12 **1107 Eleventh St.**
Bengson/Goetz
Residence (1869)
LR

One of several that escaped the wrath of Clear Creek floods, this gabled brick house was originally the home of one of Golden's Swedish immigrants. Nels Bengson, a tailor by trade, arrived in Golden with several other Swedish immigrants. The small community of Swedes established the Swedish Lutheran Church north of Clear Creek on Washington Avenue.

Ida Goetz lived in this creekside home after retiring as proprietor of the Astor House Hotel. The wrap around porch added in the early 1900s is now partially enclosed; and a flat-roofed, one-story addition has been built on the west side.

Ida Goetz at her home on Eleventh Street where she retired after running the Astor House Hotel.

Charles Judkins first arrived in Golden by wagon train in 1859 at age 18; he later ran a local saloon. This is the Historic District's oldest house, built of wood before the local clay-mining and brickmaking industries had begun.

1109 Eleventh St.
Judkins Residence
(1866)

13

The L-shaped floor plan was favored by early builders, as was the clapboard siding and gable shingles. Note the "bargeboard" along the gable eaves and the decorative woodworking on the window tops. Because the front yard is full of fruit trees, it may be difficult to see the house address.

This is one of many bungalow homes built by speculative builder Oscar Nolin. The porch and foundation were made of stone conveniently retrieved from Clear Creek. Bengsen, who was a carpenter by trade, made several later additions to this home. From 1910 to 1915, Oscar Nolin built other homes nearby, at 1102 and 1106 Cheyenne St., 1100 and 1101 Illinois St., and 1006 Thirteenth St.

1119 Eleventh St.
Elmer Bengsen
Residence, (1908)

14

Like the tail wagging the dog, this historic house is joined on the north end to a row of townhouses. Note the similarities and differences of old and new. The historic home possesses Italianate features: a low hipped roof, wide eaves, and tall thin windows. The new addition echoes the old, with its brick construction, long thin windows, and low roof.

1112 - 1200 Twelfth St.
Case Residence
(1872)

15

Colorado School of Mines Brooks Field

The Orediggers' athletic field is near the creekside campsite of early arrivals who pitched their tents here in 1859.

1219 Twelfth Street - Rubey Mine Superintendent's House (1878) LR

This simple home was owned by J. W. Rubey who rented it to workers at the nearby Parfet/Rubey clay pits. Rubey was also president of the Rubey National Bank on Washington Avenue. Long-time resident William Rowe worked at the clay mines.

Parfet/Rubey Clay Pits

Photo by Susan Goldstein

The clay deposits yielded clay for three Golden brick-yards. These bricks were used to construct many homes and buildings in early Golden and in nearby towns.

White Ash Mine Memorial

A red granite marker is the gravestone for ten miners entombed in the White Ash Coal Mine. The White Ash Mine tunneled under Clear Creek and in 1889 collapsed, drowning the ten men. Their bodies were never recovered. The White Ash Mine and other local coal mines were crucial to Golden's economy, fueling the early railroad and smelter industries, and heating Golden homes.

School of Mines Research Institute (1912)

Photo by Richard Gardner

The School of Mines built this impressive facility for instruction in mining and metallurgical resources. Laboratory experiments investigated mining, metallurgy, petroleum, and fuels. The structure was demolished in 1995 because it was contaminated by toxic by-products from testing processes.

In this gabled "L" lived George K. Kimball, Golden postmaster, Golden city clerk, and Jefferson County Commissioner. The two-story brick house on its corner site has curved window tops, frequently used for their structural strength in homes built in the 1870s through the 1890s. Notice the large carriage house in back.

1123 Twelfth St.
Kimball Residence
(1876)
LR

17

This new house imitates the old, with its similar massing and floor plan, a bay window, shingled gabled ends, and turned porch posts.

1119 Twelfth St.

18

John Titus ran a dry goods store and was a partner with James Kelly in a drugstore business. Mr. Treffeisen, the local butcher, later lived in this front-gabled brick home with its full front porch. Known as the "wiener man" by local children, Treffeisen sold hot dogs from his horse-drawn cart. The cart bell is on display at the Golden Pioneer Museum (see **Tour 4)**. This Edwardian Vernacular home has a large addition in back, made in 1995.

1114 Twelfth St.
Titus Residence
(1871), **LR**

19

This Italianate home was converted into apartments with a large east addition. Its hipped roof, brick construction and thin, arched windows reveal its historic style. Note the cobblestone retaining wall and outbuilding.

1111 Twelfth St.
Whitehead residence
(1874)

20

William Jester was the original owner of this vernacular brick home. In 1879 August Hultman added the wing and upper half story. Joseph Dennis who ran a local grocery store and livery barn lived here for several years. Dennis also served as sheriff, city alderman, and justice of the peace. It was he who applied a new brick facing in 1913.

1106 Twelfth St.
Dennis Residence
(1873)
LR

21

22 **1105 Twelfth St.**
Welch Residence
(1874)

An influential early citizen, Charles Welch was a territorial legislator and donated land for the original School of Mines east of Golden. He also sold to Adolph Coors the land where the brewery now stands. In the 1930s Golden High School principal Hugh Beers lived here. An enclosed entrance added in the mid-1900s obscures the home's traditional lines.

23 **1210 Illinois St.**
West Residence
(1902)

Prominent resident George West built this brick and shingle Dutch Colonial Revival home for his later years. This style, distinguished by the four-sided, barn-like roof was popular

throughout the state in the early 1900s. Later, Reverend Carl Wild, chaplain of First Colorado Calvary, resided here. Sam Ellis, manager of O. T. Ellis Dry Goods Store, purchased this house in 1927 and lived here with his wife for many years.

24 **1100 Thirteenth St.**
Robinson residence
(1924)

This bungalow was built by Fred B. Robinson, who owned a Washington Street book and stationery store and lived here for 35 years. bungalows like this proliferated across the country in the teens and twenties. The clipped gables, low sloping roof, wide roof overhangs, and multi-paned windows are bungalow-style elements.

Photo by Susan Goldstein

A long, low two-story building of beige brick, this is an example of the plain and utilitarian style of the 1940s and '50s. Up the hill, Coolbaugh Hall at Illinois and Fourteenth exhibits the same beige-brick linearity.

1221 Illinois St. **25**
Golden Willow
Apartments
(c. 1940s)

This stylish residence was updated by local builder Oscar Nolin in the 1910s. The original center gable is now flanked by two smaller pointed ones. It was built as the home of Jonothan H. Bradway, one

1220 Cheyenne St. **26**
Bradway residence
(1874)

of Golden's many black-smiths. Harlan Johnson, a professor at Colorado School of Mines, lived here in the 1930s and '40s. It still retains tall, arched windows, a door transom, and a lovely bay window.

This was a run-down brick house when it was remodeled in 1995 by Mark Donelson for his architectural office, with an apartment upstairs. Donelson built the second story over the north wing and put on a decorative wood porch. The one-story north wing and back section were added in the early 1900s.

1211 Cheyenne St. **27**
Business office and
apartment
(c. 1890s)

According to the present owner, this building was originally a dairy, then served as a church hall and, later, a plumbing shop. The health food store has been here since 1978, a modern version of the neighborhood grocery stores popular at the turn-of-the-century in Golden.

1205 Cheyenne St. **28**
Golden Natural Foods

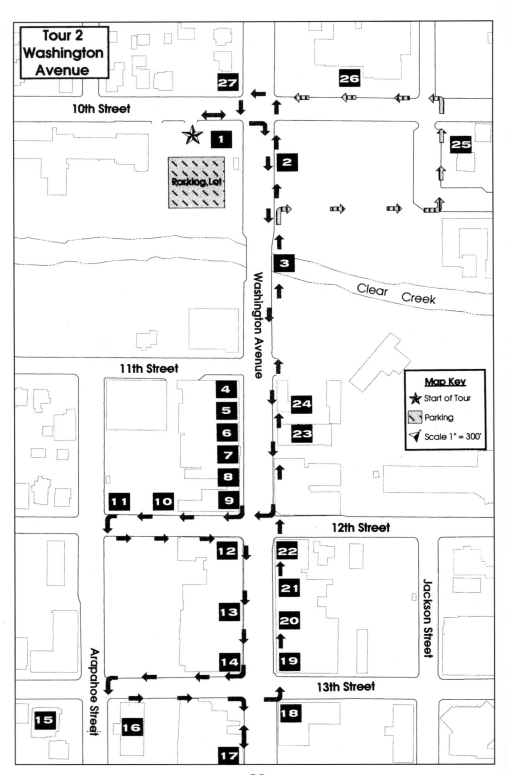

Tour 2
Washington Avenue

10th Street

★ 1

Parking Lot

27

26

25

2

3

Clear Creek

Washington Avenue

11th Street

4
5
6
7
8
9

24
23

Map Key

★ Start of Tour

Parking

Scale 1" = 300'

11   10

12th Street

22
21
20
19

12

13

14

Arapahoe Street

Jackson Street

13th Street

15

16

18

17

Tour 2	1	1000 Tenth
	2	Parfet Park
Washington	3	Washington Avenue Bridge
Avenue	4	1110 Washington
	5	1100/1102 Washington
	6	1104-1106 Washington, **LR**
	7	1116 Washington
	8	1120 Washington
	9	1122 Washington **NR**, **LR**
	10	810 Twelfth
	11	822 Twelfth, **NR**
	12	1200 Washington
	13	1212-1220 Washington
	14	1228 Washington
	15	805 Thirteenth, **NR**
	16	1301 Arapahoe, **NR**
	17	1310 Washington
	18	1301 Washington
	19	1299 Washington
	20	1211-1215 Washington
	21	1201 Washington
	22	Twelfth & Washington
	23	1111 Washington
	24	1101 Washington
	25	622 Water (optional), **LR**
	26	710 Tenth, **LR**
	27	922 Washington

NR = National Register
LR = Local Register

Photo by Susan Goldstein

- 21 -

Tour 2 Washington Avenue
TIME 1 hour   DISTANCE 1.5 miles

TIPS   Fully wheelchair/stroller accessible. Park benches for resting. Restaurants and shops for snacks and beverages. Public restrooms along tour route.

As Golden grew, so did its commercial district, Washington Avenue. False-fronted wood structures were replaced by buildings of brick. Architecture on Golden's "Main Street" ranges from the ornate 1800s commercial blocks to the 1920s beige-brick storefronts to the modern-styled buildings of recent years.

Revitalized in 1992 through a $2.2 million streetscaping project, Washington Avenue offers wide, pedestrian-pleasing sidewalks, flower-filled planters constructed of native red sandstone, Victorian street lamps, and well-placed benches. Donations from local residents and businesses made this transformation possible, and donors' names are engraved in sidewalk bricks and bench plaques.

Photo courtesy of Golden Pioneer Museum

This photo of the Golden Chamber women shows that the town was aiming to become a tourist destination.

In earlier years, the streetcar brought city folks to Golden for a day trip. The town is still a destination for residents of Denver and nearby suburbs, with dining at Washington Avenue's fine restaurants, shopping at boutiques, and visits to local museums. Multi-generation businesses like Foss Drug, Plummer Jewelry, Meyers Hardware, and The Fair 5 & 10 store have been traditional downtown anchors. Newer businesses also entice people to spend time in Golden, and residents and visitors alike are entertained by festivals such as Buffalo Bill Days, Territorial Days, Golden Fest, and the Christmas House Tour.

This new center gives a warm western welcome to the 1.5 million people who visit Golden each year. This splendid facility was built in 1996 with $250,000 in contributions from local residents and businesses. The beautiful two-story building with its Victorian style tower houses the Golden Chamber of Commerce, a reception space with brochures, maps and videos, and several conference rooms.

1000 Tenth St. **1**
Golden Visitors Center
(1996)

Beneath a gigantic cottonwood in Parfet Park is a small boulder marking the site where George West built the Boston Company store in 1859. This marker was placed here by the Daughters of the American Revolution who fought valiantly but unsuccessfully to preserve the two-story log structure. The Daughters of the America Revolution has run the Golden Pioneer Museum on Tenth Street (see **Tour 4**) for several decades.

Parfet Park **2**
Historic Marker

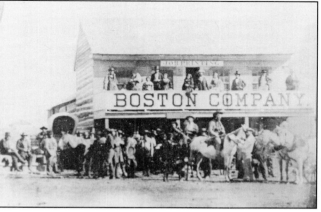

Photo courtesy of Colorado Historical Society

Early pioneers paid to cross the toll bridge built by John Ferrell in 1859. Ferrell built a foot bridge and later widened it to accommodate freight wagons and livestock. The rushing waters of Clear Creek have had a strong influence on Golden industry - early sawmills, flour mills, smelters, and Coors Brewery were all built along its banks. The bridge also offers a view of the Coors plant to the east and Mount Zion with the School of Mines **"M"** to the west.

Washington Avenue **3**
Bridge

The Howdy Folks Arch is perhaps Golden's best recognized landmark. Lu Holland was head of the Chamber of Commerce and owner of the Holland House (now the Table Mountain Inn, **#17** on this tour) when the Chamber spearheaded construction of the arch in 1949 for a cost of $7,500.

1110 Washington **4**
Howdy Folks Arch
(1949)

TIP Looking at at the buildings on the opposite side of Washington Avenue gives you a view of the historically intact upper stories.

5 **1100/1102 Washington**
Elmus Smith Grocery/
Woods Mortuary and
Crematory
(1872)
LR

Among the best preserved buildings on Washington Avenue, these two adjoining storefronts feature brick corbeling and dentils along the roof cornice. Like other downtown buildings, the street-level facade has been modernized while the second story remains historically authentic. Woods Mortuary has occupied this location for over 80 years.

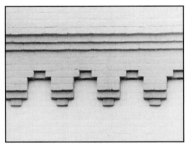

Photo courtesy of Golden Pioneer Museum

6 **1104-1106 Washington**
E. T. Osborne Store/
Odd Fellows Hall
(1872)
LR

Behind the extensively remodeled facade is the historic IOOF lodge on the second floor. The Golden Lodge #13 of the International Order of Odd Fellows was one of several fraternities once active in Golden. The lodge has met in the second floor of this building for over 100 years. On the ground level is the Washington Avenue outlet for Meyers Hardware, a local business for several decades.

7 **1116 Washington**
The Fair 5 & 10

Site of a longtime Golden variety store, this beige-brick storefront with its red-brick trim is typical of commercial architecture of the 1920s, '30s, and '40s. An earlier building located on this site had a dressmaking business on the second floor.

THE FAIR, DEALER IN
Millinery, Notions, Ladies' Gents,
and Children' Underwear, Also
Ladies' Gents, and Childrens'
Fine Shoes. The best goods for the
Least money possible.

This two-story storefront was one of many Colorado saloons built by Adolph Coors as outlets for his beer. This practice was prohibited when a post-Prohibition law banned breweries from selling their "wet goods" in such taverns. In the early 1980s, however, a Colorado entrepreneur succeeded in changing this law and established the Wynkoop Brewery in Lower Downtown Denver, kicking off an explosion of small breweries and brewpubs around the state. By the 1990s, Colorado led the nation in the number of micro-breweries. Later this building became the Treffeisen Meat Market.

1120 Washington **8**
Coors Building
(1906)

One of Colorado's most historic buildings, this two-story brick structure was originally known as the Loveland Block, and the Territorial Legislature met here in the late 1860s. Its owner, W. A. H. Loveland, was an influential force in establishing the Colorado Central Railroad headquartered in Golden. Loveland was also a territorial legislator, town treasurer, and original trustee for the Colorado School of Mines. He owned the Rocky Mountain News and the Denver Post.

1122 Washington **9**
W. A. H. Loveland
Building/ Territorial
Capital
(1863)
NR, LR

The Loveland Building housed a series of stores, including the Koenig Grocery. The names of Golden men enlisted in the armed services were painted on its side in the early 1900s.

In 1992, an $800,000 restoration made the building the anchor of the downtown district when the architectural firm of Andrews & Anderson returned it to

Photo courtesy of Denver Public Library

The Loveland Building dominated Washington Avenue in this early photograph.

its 1920s appearance. The deteriorating brick was painted a rust color while the arched windows with their "keystones" were kept intact. By 1991, it housed the Silverheels Restaurant, with the architectural offices of Andrews & Anderson upstairs.

10	**810 Twelfth St.**	The historic site of the Central Fire House, which in later
	Central Fire House/	years also housed the city hall offices, is now occupied by a
	Public Restrooms	public restroom made of native sandstone.

11	**822 Twelfth St.**
	Astor House Hotel
	Museum
	(1867)
	NR

This three-story stone hotel looks much as it did in the early days. In the late 1800s, Golden had nearly a dozen "houses," so called because they were smaller than hotels and offered home-like comfort to visitors, miners, railroad workers, unmarried male laborers, and women traveling alone. Built by Seth Lake in "frontier Georgian" style, the structure is believed to be the oldest stone hotel in the state. Deacon Lake was remembered for waking his guests by vigorously ringing a bell or ascending the stairs and shouting "Get up, get up, breakfast is ready!"

In 1897, with the help of her friends, Ida Goetz purchased the Astor House at a tax sale and ran it for several decades as a boarding house. The historic structure was saved from the bulldozers in 1973 by the citizens of Golden. Today it is run as a museum by the Golden Landmarks Association, with exhibits of items and artifacts of early Golden and a gift shop offering a variety of wares. The Astor House Hotel Museum also promotes local heritage through a regular series of programs, lectures, and teas.

Photo courtesy of Golden Transcript

In the 1990s, the Astor House was the site of festivities during Golden's Territorial Capital celebration.

This building was called the Everett Block; at the time, "block" was a term used for large masonry buildings. Francis E. Everett was mayor of Golden and well-known local businessman until he shot himself, following a period of despondency. At first it was thought that Everett had killed himself due to temporary insanity. The cause for his suicide was soon discovered — Everett had defrauded bank depositors, losing thousands of dollars in bad mining investments.

1200 Washington **12**
Everett Block
(1873)

The building's round-arched windows feature a keystone similar to those on the Loveland Building. Decorative brickwork embellishes the cornice of this attractive edifice. In front of the Everett Block is the graceful clock donated to the city by the Golden Lions Club.

Striped window awnings add a historic touch to the modernized facade of the historic Opera House. Any respectable Colorado town had to have an opera house, and this was Golden's pride and joy. Upstairs, townsfolk were entertained by band concerts, theater troupes, traveling lectures, and balls. The Opera House also was site of early School of Mines graduations, a roller skating rink, political rallies, and a dancing school. Businesses such as H. W. Pettibone and Co. Grocers, the Opera House Restaurant, and Sarell's Hardware Store were located on the first floor.

1212-1220 Washington **13**
Golden Opera
House/Ace Hi Tavern
(1879)

Photo courtesy of Denver Public Library

The arch-topped windows of the Opera House are visible in the background of this 1890s photo by Charles Ryland, showing decorated wagons enroute to Denver's Festival of Mountain and Plains.

14 **1228 Washington**
Foss Drug
(1913)

Henry and Dorothy Foss bought H. Langenhan's drugstore in 1913. Henry, and later his son Heinie, expanded the business into a huge emporium that lives up to its slogan "Where the West Shops." A mammoth Art Deco-style parapet echoes the

style of the original building, which began as a 25-foot-wide structure on Washington Avenue. On the south side, where once stood the Denver-Interurban streetcar depot, is a mural by artist Robert Dafford, depicting historic Golden with horse-drawn wagons, the streetcar, early automobiles, and several early landmarks.

Corner of Thirteenth & Washington on Armistice Day,
November 11, 1918

15 **805 Thirteenth St.**
Calvary Episcopal
Church
(1867)
NR

This is the state's oldest continuously-used Episcopal church. Early church members included three of Golden's most influential people: George West, Edward Berthoud, and W. A. H. Loveland. Loveland was church treasurer and donated a considerable amount of funds to build "the finest church in the territory." Calvary Episcopal also helped establish the territorial college that was a forerunner of the School of Mines.

The brick church is Gothic Revival style, characterized by pointed-arch windows, a steep-sloping roof, and carved roof brackets. Tours of the interior are available by inquiring at the church office next door. From the church entry way is an enchanting view of Golden with the backdrop of North Table Mountain.

This 1873 photo shows the Golden Hotel and Calvary
Episcopal Church

This was the historic site of the Golden Hotel, the city's finest lodging when it was built in 1870. The three-story structure burned down eight years after it was built.

1301 Arapahoe
Armory Building
(1913)
NR

Constructed the same year as the original Foss Drug building, the Armory is believed to be the largest cobblestone structure west of the Mississippi. James Gow was the architect and contractor who supplied the cannonball-sized stones from Clear Creek and Golden Gate Canyon. Gow also constructed the Castle Rock pavilion (see **Tour 5**) and the county jail. The Armory was headquarters for

When first built, the Armory Building housed the Golden Post Office on the ground floor.

the ROTC unit active at the Colorado School of Mines during World War I and II.

This lodging has had several incarnations, beginning as the Berrimoor Hotel, then becoming the LaRay Hotel. In the late 1940s, Lu Holland remodeled it as the Holland House Motel and Restaurant. In 1992, a $2.9 million renovation of the vacant structure helped revitalize downtown Golden. This ren-

1310 Washington
Holland House/Table Mountain Inn
(1924-25)

ovation was accomplished through low-cost loans, a block grant from the Colorado Office of Business Development, and the investments of Boulder restaurateur Frank Day and local partner Bart Bortles, the former owner of Golden Eagle Saloon. Now, the hotel is designed in Pueblo Revival style with pale stucco exterior, wood vigas, and clay-tile roof.

In the late 1800s, Golden had nearly a dozen hotels and inns like the historic Avenue Hotel shown above.

18   **1301 Washington**
Gem Theater/
Steve's Corner
(1912)

A rearing black stallion marks the entrance of this western-wear shop, however a stepped parapet facade reveals the building's early origins as the Gem Theater. The Golden Athletic Club was once also located here. Inside are an antique movie projector and other historic memorabilia.

19   **1299 Washington**
Linder Hardware/
Hested's Department
Store
(1957, 1962)

On the site of the historic Linder Hardware store stands a rather modern building. This long, low red brick store front acquired its white facade and wavy roof overhang in 1962, typical features of '60s commercial style.

20   **1211 - 1215 Washington**
Garbarino, Poe,
Crawford, and
Avenue Hotels

These buildings were at various times historic hotels and associated restaurants and taverns. 1215 Washington once housed a portion of Linder Hardware. The beige-brick facades are typical of the 1920s, '30s, and '40s.

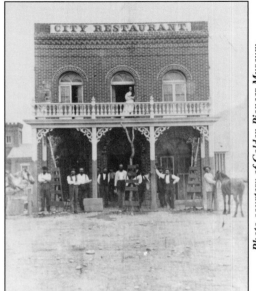

Photo courtesy of Golden Pioneer Museum

In the 1870s, the City Restaurant occupied this site.

21   **1201 Washington**
Smith Block/Rubey
National Bank/First
National Bank
(1873)

After a 1901 renovation, this storefront was called the "handsomest building in town." It housed the bank owned by Jesse W. Rubey, who was a two-term Golden mayor. The brick building is embellished with ornate pilasters and window tops, and a frieze decorated with swags and garlands. The Washington and Twelfth intersection was the crossroads of Golden. Here a forty-foot-tall flagpole was located for many years, serving as a focal point of the community. It was the site of bonfires and other celebrations, and where Santa Claus arrived when he came to visit Golden children.

This conglomeration of now-connected storefronts has contained a variety of businesses: a harness shop, confectionery, Chinese laundry, jewelry store, telegraph office, cigar manufacturer, Golden Woodmen Lodge, and clothing store. At one time the Buick Auto Garage had a glass-windowed showroom large enough to display one car. By the 1980s, the Buffalo Rose Dance Hall occupied the former Golden recreation center — the swimming pool is still in the basement. This site was also the location of the historic Overland Hotel.

The historic origins of the buildings are evidenced by the exposed brick wall interiors. The "boom town" facades were added in the 1980s.

Photo courtesy of Golden Pioneer Museum

old OVERlANd HoTEl Abou† 1900.

Historic Overland Hotel on Washington Ave.

Twelfth and Washington, ne
(c. 1870s & 1880s)
Buffalo Rose Dance Hall Sportsman's Barbershop, and Kenrows Restaurant

22

The Center is home to the Rocky Mountain Quilt Museum, which showcases the handiwork of early pioneers as well as contemporary artists from around the state and the country. The Center's brick construction, two-story height, and conforming setback help this newer building blend in with its older neighbors. Corbeling and dentils at the cornice create an historic atmosphere furthered by the atrium, wood oak trim, and brass chandeliers inside.

1111 Washington
Golden Center

23

Photo courtesy of Golden Pioneer Museum

Although greatly altered, this structure was significant in early Golden history. It was built by George West and Dr. James Kelly. The doctor ran his pharmacy downstairs and George West published the Colorado Transcript upstairs. The building's original size and scale are intact.

1101 Washington
Colorado Transcript Office/Kelly Drug Store
(1870)

24

25 **622 Water St.**
(optional)
Barnes/Peery
Residence,
(1865)
LR

East of Parfet Park on Water Street is an Italianate house associated with Golden's early flour-milling industry. This large, brick Italianate is one of the town's oldest residences. It was the home of David Barnes Sr., who built it and the Golden Mill, which he operated until he sold it in 1878. The Peery brothers, William and Ira bought the mill in the 1900s, and for several decades members of the Peery family lived in this house. The mill still stands near Water and Ford Street.

The Italianate style popular in the U. S. in the 1850s and 1860s is evident in the low-pitched, hipped roof and wide overhang supported by paired brackets.

Photo courtesy of Golden Pioneer Museum

The Rock Flour Mill was located on Clear Creek

26 **710 Tenth St.**
Golden High
School/American
Mountaineering
Center
(1924)
LR

After years of bickering between Northsiders and Southsiders, the North Side became the location of the grand new high school designed by noted architect Eugene G. Groves and built on the former site of the Eagle Corral and stables. The local newspaper called it "the last word in high school construction." The three-story Beaux Arts school building is blond brick trimmed in terra cotta with columbines blooming at the entrance. The beige brick and the terra cotta ornamentation are elements of the Beaux Arts style.

After later serving as a junior high school, the building was treated to a $500,000 restoration and in 1994 opened as the American Mountaineering Center. Headquartered here are the Colorado Mountain Club and American Alpine Club. The center houses a mountaineering museum, a book shop, and a 300-square-foot scale model of Mount Everest. Inside, the "Dawn of the West" mural (1928) by Gerald Cassidy shows images of early Golden icons, including Native Americans, a pioneer family, and a prospector.

This was one of Golden's many grocery stores. Nankivell was a Golden mayor, and Jones was a Jefferson County treasurer; nevertheless, their business failed in the panic of 1893. The store was bought by Caleb E. Parfet and was later owned and operated by E. E. Stewart. The Knights of Pythias met on the second floor, as did the Ku Klux Klan.

The mural on the south side depicts one of the area's earliest residents — Clear Creek Valley was visited by the Arapaho, Cheyenne, and Ute tribes before American settlers arrived.

Photo courtesy of Golden Pioneer Museum

The store at 922 Washington had several different owners.

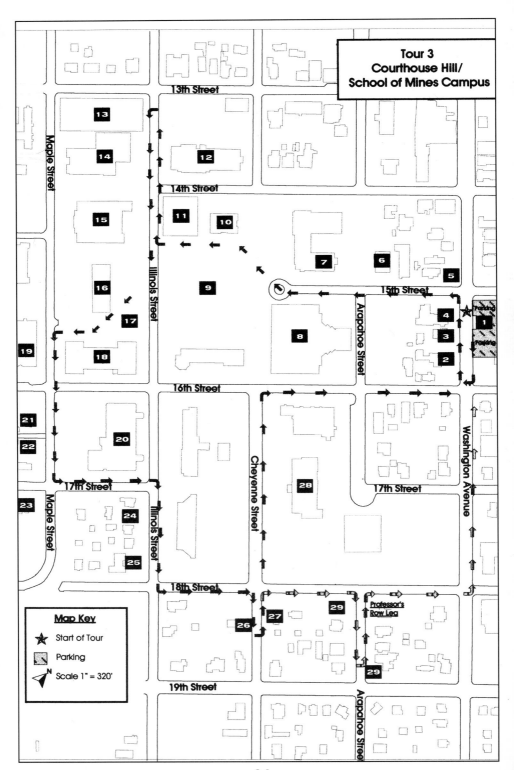

Tour 3
Courthouse Hill/
School of Mines Campus

13th Street

14th Street

Maple Street

Illinois Street

15th Street

Arapahoe Street

Washington Avenue

16th Street

17th Street

Maple Street

Cheyenne Street

17th Street

Illinois Street

18th Street

Professor's
Row Lea

Map Key

★ Start of Tour

Parking

N Scale 1" = 320'

19th Street

Arapahoe Street

Tour 3

Courthouse Hill and School of Mines Campus

1 1500 block of Washington Avenue
2 Unger/Boatright Residence, **LR**
3 Rubey Residence, **LR**
4 Foothills Art Center, **NR**
5 Broad Residence
6 Hall of Engineering
7 View of Mines M-blem
8 Green Center
9 Kadafar Commons
10 Stratton Hall
11 Chauvenet Hall
12 Coolbaugh Hall
13 Steinhauser Field House
14 Russell Volk Gymnasium
15 Arthur Lakes Library
16 Guggenheim Hall
17 Burro Sculpture
18 Berthoud Hall
19 Ben Parker Student Center
20 Van Tuyl Residence
21 Allen Residence
22 Coolbaugh House, **LR**
23 George Brown Hall
24 1704 and 1710 Illinois, **LR**
25 President's Residence
26 Parker Residence
27 Parfet Residence
28 1960s Jefferson County Courthouses
29 Optional Leg:
   Professor's Row
   Herman Frederick Coors Residence, **LR**
   Mosley Residence

NR = National Register
LR = Local Register

Courtesy Colorado School of Mines

Colorado School of Mines campus

Tour 3 Courthouse Hill/School of Mines Campus
TIME 45 minutes to 1 hour   **DISTANCE** 1 to 1.5 miles

TIPS Full wheelchair/stroller access on campus. Parts of this tour are hilly. Neighborhoods at start and end of tour may require using driveways to enter/exit sidewalks. Plenty of stopping/resting places. Restrooms at Geology Museum (# **13**).

The School of Mines has exerted an influence on Golden since its founding. Several prominent local residents were instrumental in the formation of the school. W. A. H. Loveland persuaded the legislature to locate the college in Golden, Charles C. Welch donated land for the school, and E. L. Berthoud helped establish classes. Newspaper editor George West eloquently lobbied in the *Colorado Transcript,* "What, therefore, our country wants, what Colorado and her sister Territories want, is a school of Mines convenient to the districts where the precious deposits of gold and silver, and other metals are found in such abundance. Golden City appears to be the place for such a convenience . . ."

Both Central City and Denver clamored to be the site of the mining school, but Golden received the honor in 1870, when the Territorial Legislature passed a bill establishing a School of Mines and appropriated $3,872.45 for that purpose. A mines classroom building was constructed as part of Jarvis Hall, an Episcopalian college southeast of Golden where Lookout Mountain School for Boys is located today. When a wind storm blew this structure down before it was completed, the school

Jarvis Hall, original School of Mines moved into Golden on five acres donated by Charles C. Welch.

Matthews Hall   *Jarvis Hall*   *School of Mines*

Photo courtesy of Colorado School of Mines

From its beginning, the School of Mines promoted Colorado's mining industry. Experimental testing of Colorado coal by first Mines president E. J. Mallett (1871 - 1875) proved the effectiveness of this resource as fuel for smelters and steam engines, boosting industry throughout the state. The most popular early course was fire assaying, a technique used to evaluate the gold and silver content of ore. In the 1890s, the school administration ceased granting "Assay Diplomas," instead encouraging students to enroll in a degree program.

As a world-class school today, CSM has "the largest enrollment and is the second oldest institution (after Columbia University's School of Mines, 1864) in the United States emphasizing minerals, materials science, and energy engineering education," according to the pamphlet *In the Mines Tradition: 1995 - 1996*. Tours of Rocky Mountain mines, as well as the Edgar Mine that the school operates in Idaho Springs, give students hands-on experience in the mining industry. Annual enrollment averages 3,000 undergraduate and graduate students.

Photo courtesy of Colorado School of Mines

Like other universities, CSM has its traditions and rituals. In earlier years, these included a freshmen-versus-seniors tug of war across Clear Creek, homecoming raft races on the creek, and the wearing of cowboy hats being reserved for seniors. A ritual still observed is the annual white-washing of the School of Mines **"M"** high on Mount Zion, done in fall by the incoming freshmen class and in springtime by the outbound seniors. The mascot is still the prospector's burro, honored by a bronze statue visited on this tour. And the "Orediggers" still sing, to the tune of an old English drinking song:

Geology and mineralogy students in the early 1900s

"I'm a rambling wreck from Golden Tech, a hell of an engineer. . . A shooting, fighting, dynamiting, mining engineer."

The 1878 Jefferson County Courthouse - this is a colorized postcard printed in 1907.

Photo courtesy of Colorado School of Mines

1 **1500 Washington**
Site of historic Jefferson County Courthouse
(1878)

Traditionally the School of Mines shared the hill with the Jefferson County courthouse. Several prominent Goldenites made their homes across the street from the courthouse.

The Jefferson County Courthouse built in 1878 on this site was demolished in the 1960s, replaced by a new courthouse and Hall of Justice, visited at the end of this tour. The current courthouse is a massive post-modern structure built on the ridge southeast of Golden.

2 **1518 Washington**
Unger Residence/ Boatright Residence
(c. 1905)

According to *The Foothills Art Center* by Toni L. Scheunemann, Perre O. Unger built this distinguished-looking foursquare for his family. Unger was a successful local contractor responsible for many Washington Avenue commercial buildings as well as several private residences in the early 1900s. In 1910 Unger sold the

house to William L. Boatright, who was District Attorney (1920 - 1925) and Colorado Attorney General (1925 - 1929). Boatright was also active in water rights cases and a fervent advocate of prohibition. Notable for its shingled dormers and leaded glass windows, the house was converted to a restaurant and gift shop in the 1980s.

This Edwardian Vernacular home was the first residence built on Courthouse Hill, constructed by Perre Unger as a "speculative home." It was later purchased by Jesse and Ella Rubey. Mr. Rubey, a mayor of Golden and partner in the Woods-Rubey National Bank on Washington Avenue, paid $3,250 for the house.

1510 Washington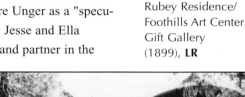
Rubey Residence/
Foothills Art Center
Gift Gallery
(1899), **LR**

The painted brick home features a round tower, bands of small wood dentils, and a wrap-around porch supported by classic columns and topped by fanciful finials. A small, shingled porch peeps down from the second story.

The Gothic Revival style church features pointed-arch windows and a pointed-arch entranceway. Its square bell tower, built in 1898 by George Kimball, James Gow, and H. H. Linder and Company, is adorned with corbeling, small brick pointed arches, and a whimsical finial. Connected to the church is the Queen Anne-style parsonage built by Gow. Its massive, shingled roof and onion-domed tower shelter the work of artists in all media.

809 Fifteenth St. **4**
First Presbyterian
Church (1872) and
Rectory (1892)/
Foothills Art Center
Gift Gallery
NR

The church was bought for $30,000 in 1970 to become a "living art center," and Irma Whys was the center's first volunteer director. Regular events include the Rocky Mountain Watermedia Exhibit, North American Sculpture Exhibition, Clayfest, and Holiday Art Market.

Photo courtesy of Golden Pioneer Museum

***The historic church and parsonage were converted
into the Foothills Art Center in the 1970s.***

5 **1422 Washington**
Richard Broad
Residence
(1879)
LR

This abundantly shingled Queen Anne became the Antique Rose Bed and Breakfast in the 1990s. Its history reveals how an owner could alter a home's appearance by updating a plain, vernacular dwelling with Queen Anne features.

Grace A. Sales bought this lot in 1879 and built a house upon

it. The next owner was Alice Clark, wife of Charles T. Clark, who owned the house from 1888 to 1895. Richard Broad, Jefferson County Commissioner and state senator, bought the house in 1895 and extensively remodeled it between 1895 and 1906. Broad also managed Colorado enterprises for the Guggenheim family. Another addition was put on in 1910, and the house was sold in 1945 for $1,000.

Photo courtesy of Colorado School of Mines

Copied from the scrapbook of School of Mines student,
this picture shows that engineering students
knew how to have a little fun.

Colorado School of Mines Campus

After visiting Courthouse Hill, the tour now continues on to the School of Mines campus. The campus architecture ranges from the 1894 brick-and-stone Hall of Engineering to Mission Style buildings with curvilinear parapets to the sleek brick-and-glass structures of modern design. As is customary, building dedications honor notable Mines trustees, benefactors, presidents, and professors.

The campus portion of **Tour 3** begins with the oldest building at the School of Mines and proceeds through the campus to a residential neighborhood at the end.

The oldest structure on campus, this three-story schoolhouse is of brick and stone with sandstone trim at the round entry arch and foundation. Arched windows in trios and pairs, elaborate brick corbels, and a stepped parapet highlight this stylish building. It was designed by Robert S. Roeschlaub, who prepared the campus design plan and was architect for the Central City Opera House and numerous historic Denver schools.

816 Fifteenth **6**
Hall of Engineering
(1894)

Photo courtesy of Colorado School of Mines

Photo courtesy of Colorado School of Mines

Walking westward along Fifteenth, you can see the School of Mines **"M"** on Mount Zion.

View of Mines **7**
"M-blem"
(1908)

8 **Fifteenth &
Arapahoe, nw**
Cecil H. and Ida
Green Graduate and
Professional Center
(1972)

This modern, immense beige-brick facility is named for a Mines student who was a

founding partner in the reorganization of Geophysical Service, Inc., which created the giant corporation, Texas Instruments.

9 **Kadafar Commons**

Nicknamed "the Quad," this open, grassy square is bordered on all four sides by school buildings. Fraternity houses and the president's home were once located along Sixteenth Street, then called "College Avenue." Because there were no dormitories until the 1950s, students lodged at fraternity houses or boarding houses, or roomed with local families. A number of Mines students commuted from Denver on the streetcar line.

Courtesy Colorado School of Mines

***This photograph by Laura Gilpin shows the homes along
"College Avenue," which were razed in the 1940s for campus
expansion and development of the quadrangle.***

Guggenheim Hall (**#17** on this tour) dominates the west side of the campus. The abstract sculpture — "Of Earth and Men" by artist John T. Young — is bordered by the Simplicity Rose Garden.

This three-story building of Golden-made brick was designed by Harlan Thomas who was also the architect for several structures on the Colorado State University in Fort Collins. Its foundation was made with crushed slag from the remains of the Golden Smelting Works. The base is Lyons sandstone. The hall was the first steel-frame building on campus.

900 Fourteenth Street
Stratton Hall
(1901)

10

It is named for mining millionaire Winfield Scott Stratton, a trustee and benefactor of the school who donated $25,000 to the school in 1900. The distinctive curvilinear parapets are Mission Style and can be seen on other campus buildings of the same vintage.

These two adjoining buildings continue the Mission Style theme with their curvilinear parapet and round-arched windows and openings. Originally built as separate structures, the power plant (1902) and the fire assay building (1905) were later joined and now serve as classrooms.

Fourteenth & Illinois, se
Chauvenet Hall
(1905)

11

The Mission Style Chauvenet Hall and Stratton Hall are distinguished by the curvilinear parapets.

Built of beige brick and glass, this building was dedicated to Melville C. Coolbaugh, Mines president (1925 - 1946) and president emeritus (1946 - 1950). Its lean geometric lines are honored by the more recent addition on the north side.

Fourteenth & Illinois, ne
Coolbaugh Hall
(1952)

12

13 **Thirteenth & Illinois, sw**
Steinhauer Field House
(1937)

The hillside location makes this building difficult for access by wheelchairs and strollers, but it can be viewed from the corner of Fourteenth and Illinois. Noted architect Jules Jacques Benoit Benedict designed this beige-brick structure trimmed in brown brick. On its east side it bears a bas-relief of the Mines mascot burro and the pick-and-shovel symbol. The fieldhouse is named for Frederick C. Steinhauer who served on the board of trustees from 1911 to 1915 and from 1931 to 1947. His son, Gurnett Steinhauer, was vice president of Mines for business affairs from 1968 to 1972.

14 **Fourteenth & Illinois, nw**
Russell Volk Gymnasium
(1937)

On this site stood the brick, three-story Mission Style gymnasium, built in 1908. The newer gymnasium is named for "Rut" Volk who graduated from Mines in 1926 and received a Master of Science in Engineering degree in 1931. He served as a trustee from 1967 to 1973. As a student he earned 15 letters as a Mines athlete.

15 **Fourteenth & Illinois, sw**
Arthur Lakes Library
(1954)

This beige-brick building, with its red tile roof, blends well with the older campus structures. Its namesake was known as the "Father of Colorado Geology." Professor Lakes was on the Mines faculty from 1874 to 1893. He collected fossil, rock, and mineral specimens, many of which are on display at the museum next door in Berthoud Hall.

The specialized technical library contains over 145,000 volumes, 175,000 maps, and 2,000 magazines and journals. The Mining History Archives were created in 1995 with a donation from Russell and Lynn Wood. Inside the library are framed watercolors of dinosaurs and local geological formations, and the Frank C. Allison gold and silver specimen exhibit, presented to CSM by the Boettcher family in 1937.

Architect James Murdoch designed this administration building, which was financed with $80,000 donated by smelter magnate and U. S. Senator

1500 Illinois St.
Guggenheim Hall
(1905)

Photo courtesy of Colo. School of Mines

Simon Guggenheim to celebrate the birth of his son. For several decades, the Guggenheim family dominated the smelting industry in Colorado. A small, gold-domed cupola atop a square bell tower distinguishes the three-story gray brick building, which has been restored as the campus centerpiece. Around Golden, the bells can be heard chiming on the hour.

Featuring two burros laden with prospect gear, this sculpture by Robin J. Laws is called "A Friend to Lean On." It was funded by the Adolph Coors Foundation in 1995.

Illinois St.
Burro Sculpture

This four-story hall, built as a WPA project, is flanked by two-story wings and roofed in red tile. It was designed by well-known Denver architect Temple Hoyne Buell. Entry surrounds, pilasters, and wide, double-bracketed eaves are lavishly trimmed in terra cotta in exuberant Beaux Arts detail.

Berthoud Hall
**Sixteenth &
Illinois, nw**
(1938)

The building bears the name of Edward R. Berthoud, one of Golden's earliest and most influential citizens. Berthoud surveyed the original town plat in

Photo courtesy of Colo. School of Mines

1860 and influenced construction of the toll road. He was later involved with surveying and constructing the railroad up Clear Creek Canyon. He was on the original School of Mines board of trustees and taught civil engineering classes when the school opened. His headstone in the Golden cemetery reads "Explorer, Pioneer, Soldier, Scientist."

Tip: Cross to east side for wheelchair access.

Site #18, continued - Ore carts, boulders, and snarling terra cotta lion heads mark the northern entrance to the Mines Geological Museum, in Berthoud Hall. The museum features fossils, minerals, gemstones, and gold specimens from around the world. Children may take a free ore sample from the ore cart in front of the building.

Photo by Susan Goldstein

19 | **Maple & Sixteenth, nw**
Ben Parker Student Center
(1964, addition 1996)

A geometric glass-and-metal atrium marks the entrance of this modern building. Parker was the first Mines graduate to become president (1946-1950). He was a trustee from 1950 to 1969. His home is near the end of this tour.

20 | **1207 Sixteenth St.**
Van Tuyl Residence
(1905)

This side-gabled Dutch Colonial Revival building was home of Francis Van Tuyl, head of CSM geology department. Distinguished by three pedimented dormers above a massive columned porch, it now serves as a fraternity house. In the school's early years, students lodged in nearly a dozen such fraternity houses.

21 | **1616 Maple**
Allen Residence
(1900)

This front-gabled Dutch Colonial Revival was originally the home of George Allen, football coach and head of Mines physical education department. Professor Merton Signer later lived here. Today it is the office for the Minority Engineering Program. It is one of three Dutch Colonial Revival homes clustered near the corner of Maple and Sixteenth.

These two Dutch Colonial style homes are near the intersection of Maple and Sixteenth Streets.

Photo by Susan Goldstein

The Coolbaugh House now contains the Mines University Club. Its Craftsman-style influences are seen its story-and-a-half height, cross-gabled roof, timbered porch gable, and prominent brick chimney.

1700 Maple
Coolbaugh House
(1920)
LR

22

This sleek, curvilinear building exhibits the round corners and ribbon windows favored by modern design and made possible by twentieth century construction technology. Brown was a 1922 graduate who received the Distinguished Achievement Medal in 1949. He developed Brown & Root from a small road building firm to one of the world's largest engineering and construction conglomerates.

Sixteenth & Illinois, sw
George R. Brown Geology Hall
(1979)

23

Peaked gables, beige and brown brick, and arched entrance ways mark these English/ Norman Cottages. Homes of this popular style can be seen elsewhere on campus and in town. Two particularly good examples of this style are **#18** on **Tour 5**, the East Golden Tour.

1704 Illinois (1914)
LR &1710 Illinois
(1936)

24

This imposing Jacobean/Elizabethan style home is characterized by the shingled roof with flared gables, casement windows, and timbering. It has served as the University Club and as the Sigma Nu Fraternity. The residence was designed by Burnham and Merrill Hoyt; Burnham Hoyt also designed Red Rocks Amphitheater and many notable Denver public buildings.

1722 Illinois
Colorado School of Mines President's Residence, (1928)

25

Ben H. Parker was a geology professor at Colorado School of Mines, Mines president (1946-1950), and member of the board of trustees. Parker's Colonial Revival home was designed by architect Donald Weese, who was director of the Mountain States Architectural Small House Service Bureau. Shuttered windows and an ornate doorway are hallmarks of this style.

1001 Eighteenth St.
Parker Residence
(1941)

26

Tip: Cross to east side for shaded sidewalk.

27	**923 Eighteenth St.** George W. Parfet Residence (1913)	This bungalow was home to the Parfet family. George W. Parfet Sr. arrived in Colorado in 1874 and, at the time of his death in 1924, ran the largest clay-mining operation in Jefferson County. His son George Jr. took over the family business and was chairman of the Jefferson County board of commissioners when he was killed by an explosion at one of the clay pits.
28	**Eighteenth & Arapahoe** Jefferson County Courthouses (1960s)	Labeled "Loveland Park" on 1800s maps, this area is occupied by the county complex built in the 1960s. In 1995 the School of Mines purchased these three former county buildings. The old sheriff/assessor's office now contains officers for the School of Mines Foundation. The Justice Hall, designed in 1965 by Robert D. Laramey, was featured on a tour of the American Institute of Architects when they held their conference in Denver in 1966.

Photo courtesy of Colorado School of Mines

Colorado School of Mines Faculty, 1894 - 1895 school year.
Clockwise from left: Arthur Ransley, Eldridge G. Moody (Librarian), Louis
Clarence Hill? (Physics and Electrical Engineering), Horace B. Patton (Geology
and Mineralogy), Clinton B. Stewart (Civil Engineering), Robert S. Stockton,
George Tilden (Chemistry), Regis Chauvenet (President),
Paul Meyer (Mathematics professor and Golden physician)
and Edmund Kirby (Metallurgy and Mining).

Courthouse Hill/School of Mines Tour - Optional Leg

1800 block of Arapaho, Professor's Row

Many Mines professors have resided on this tree-lined block, in Norman/Tudor Cottages with round-arched doorways and steeply pitched gabled entrances, and Craftsman-style homes with overhanging eaves, exposed rafters, and clipped gables.

1817 Arapahoe, Herman Frederick Coors Residence, LR (c. 1919)

The large stucco and stone home with its Gothic revival elements began as a bungalow, a portion of which is visible on the west side. Herman Frederick Coors hired Architect Jules Jacques Benoit Benedict to create this "mountain lodge," after rejecting an Italian Renaissance design by architects Fisher & Fisher. Mrs. Coors personally selected the stones that trim the exterior.

The French doors and pointed-arch windows create a light, airy feeling inside. The interior is distinguished by dark wood trim, stained-glass windows, an unusual octagonal entrance, and the stylish stone fireplace that is a signature of architect Benedict. The home was the first landmark locally designated in Golden. The stone lions on the east end of the yard were supposedly brought back by Coors from the Peruvian jungle.

922 Nineteenth Street, Mosley Residence (1903)

This gracious farmhouse was built on three lots acquired in 1902 for back taxes of $23.45. In the 1930s and '40s it was the residence of Fred and Cora Meyers, owners of Meyers Market, at that time located at 1214 Washington. The wrap-around porch, now enclosed, was added in 1905. Inside, the stairway banister and spindle-work are original. Its style is Edwardian Vernacular, as seen in the shingle-clad walls, shingled gables, and graceful porch.

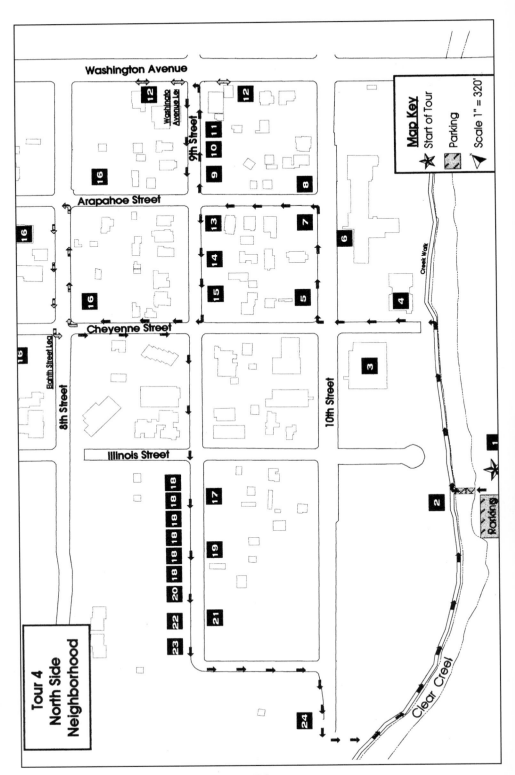

Tour 4
North Side Neighborhood

Washington Avenue

Arapahoe Street

Cheyenne Street

Illinois Street

9th Street

8th Street

Eighth Street Lead

10th Street

Washington Avenue Le

Creek Walk

Clear Creek

Parking

Map Key
★ Start of Tour
▨ Parking
Scale 1" = 320'

- 50 -

Tour 4

North Side Neighborhood

1 Clear Creek Ranch Park
2 Creekwalk
3 Golden Library
4 Golden Pioneer Museum
5 922 Tenth
6 Golden City Hall
7 900 Tenth
8 822 Tenth
9 823 Ninth
10 815 Ninth
11 807 Ninth
12 Washington Avenue leg (optional)
   908 Washington
   822 Washington
   800 Washington
   600 Ninth Street
13 900 Arapahoe
14 911 Ninth
15 921-923 Ninth
16 Eighth Street leg (optional)
   Eighth and Cheyenne
   Eighth and Arapahoe
   714 Cheyenne, **SR**
17 1013 Ninth Street
18 1100 - 1160 Ninth
19 1145 Ninth
20 1170 Ninth
21 1180-1190 Ninth
22 1200 Ninth, **LR**
23 Lions Park
24 Golden Community Center

Photo courtesy Golden Pioneer Museum

The Golden Milling Company was one of Golden's three mills and one of several industries located in the North Side neighborhood.

Tour 4 North Side Tour

TIME 1 to 1.5 hour　　　　　　　**DISTANCE** 1.5 to 2 miles

TIPS　The North Side is a flat, shady neighborhood. Two optional legs take you to restaurants and other sites. Restrooms are at the end of the tour, west of Lions Park **#24**). Some parts of the tour may require using driveways to enter/exit sidewalks.

The availability of water for industrial purposes was key to the growth of Golden. Clear Creek provided water for an early sawmill, flour mills, the Golden Paper Mill, early breweries, and a number of smelters. Most of these enterprises were located north of the creek, and the North Side grew as a working-class neighborhood. North Side residents worked at the Black Diamond and White Ash coal mines, for the railroads, and at the mills, such as the Golden Mill, which produced "Pride of the West" flour and sold hay, grain, and feed. Local clay deposits contributed to the thriving brickyards, pottery works, and porcelain plant north of the creek.

While Clear Creek contributed to local industry, it also divided the town geographically and socially. This rivalry probably began when the Boston Company and W. A. H. Loveland raced to complete the first commercial structure in Golden City. Loveland won, but only because he "borrowed" roof shingles from the competition. The antagonism between the "Northsiders" and "Southsiders" waged for years, culminating in the 1920s when the new High School was built on the north side at Tenth and

Courtesy Golden Pioneer Museum

Miners in the White Ash Coal Mine once located north of Clear Creek.

Washington (**#26** on **Tour 2**).

In the early 1900s, Clear Creek was wide and sprawling.

The history of the North Side residents often went unrecorded in the local newspapers. Some residents were miners from Gilpin County who moved here during the decline of mining in the 1870s and again in the 1900s. Others were German immigrants who settled east of Washington Avenue. Nearly all residents, however, worked at businesses on the North Side. The legacy of these early Goldenites is the collection of vernacular homes, notable for their simplicity of style.

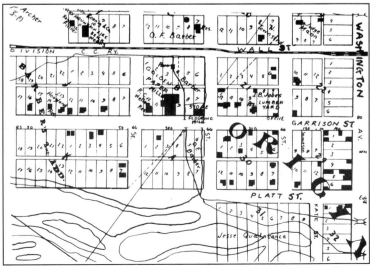

This 1878 map shows the Golden Paper Mills, Flouring Mill, and B. Jobes Lumber Yard along Ninth Street (at that time called Garrison Street).

To the north, along Wall Street (now Eighth Street) is where the Rocky Mountain Fire Brick Works and the railroad were located.

- 53 -

1 **900 - 1100 Eleventh St.**
Clear Creek Ranch Park
(1990s)

Two log cabins, a schoolhouse, and a barn at this creekside site were brought from Golden Gate canyon as examples of the area's earliest building types. Built in the 1870s, the story-and-a-half Thomas Pearce Cabin was actually moved twice — once when it was bought in the 1930s by Pearce who took apart the ax-hewn logs, numbered them, then re-assembled the cabin on his ranch. It was again relocated, to its present site in 1994 in the Clear Creek Ranch Park run by the Golden Landmarks Association.

This family portrait was taken in front of a cabin at White Ranch west of Golden.

The smaller cabin is believed to have been built by Mrs. Reynolds who homesteaded next to the Pearce Ranch. In early days, settlers often moved cabins in order to re-use building materials.

2 **Creekwalk**

The Creekwalk extends east to near the Coors Brewery and west to the campground at the west end of Tenth Street. Clear Creek sustains local wildlife, including beaver and water fowl.

3 **1019 Tenth St.**
Golden Library
(1961)

The new library, which opened in 1996 in the renovated recreation center (architects Andrews and Anderson), contains a collection of books on Golden history and railroad history. The library began in a woodframe building near Thirteenth and Jackson Streets, organized in the early 1900s by local women. Looking east from the library parking lot, you can see the tracks of the Castle Rock Scenic Railway that ran up the north face of Castle Rock in the 1910s. (See **Tour 5).**

4 **923 Tenth St.**
Golden DAR Pioneer Museum
(1970)

The Daughters of the American Revolution have helped keep history alive in Golden for decades. After an unsuccessful attempt to save George West's Boston Company building, they established a museum adjoining the Golden City Hall. A move in 1996 gave this wonderful collection of items a creekside home in the former public library.

This tiny clapboard house is typical of homes found in the North Side neighborhood. Various additions were made to it over the years. Next door at 918 Tenth is a similar dwelling, a two-storied clapboard with diamond shingles in the gable end. These and other small North Side homes resemble the shotgun miner's homes in mining towns like Central City.

922 Tenth St.
(1870s)

5

Photo by Cathleen Norman

Golden's beige-brick city hall, across the street on the south side of Tenth Street, was built in the early 1960s. In front of it is the Liberty Bell, originally the fire alarm bell at the Central Fire House on Twelfth Street. The bell was rung so hard on Armistice Day (November 11, 1918) that its clapper cracked. Beside it is the Golden Gardeners' rose garden in honor of Stella Rall, the first president of that club.

911 Tenth St.
Golden City Hall
(1961)

6

This one-and-a-half-story clapboard home is distinguished by a wide frieze board, and ornate roof brackets. It was the home of William W. Gayton, who was listed as owning a "Baled Hay" business in the 1878 Golden Business Directory and who also owned three other houses nearby.

900 Tenth St.
Gayton Residence
(1879)

7

This sketch of the home at 900 Tenth Street is from the Golden Globe.

8 **822 Tenth St.**
E. E. and Mattie
Stewart
Residence
(pre-1873)

The Stewarts, who were proprietors of Stewart Grocery at Ninth and Washington, lived in this small brick home two blocks from their business. Next door, at 816 and 810 Tenth are other brick vernacular homes typical of Golden's early working folk.

9 **823 Ninth St.**

This cross-gabled brick home possesses arched windows and arched window sashes. The setback, the two-story height, and the similar color of the modern addition help it to blend with the original structure.

10 **815 Ninth St.**

The brick sidewalk, spindle-work screen door, and flower garden give a Victorian air to this clapboard cottage. It sits next to Church Ditch, named for William Churches, who was the early developer of the ditch. It is one of three irrigation ditches that siphoned water from Clear Creek to cultivate local crops and gardens.

11 **807 Ninth St.**
Faragher Residence/
Stage Stop (1880)

Originally a clapboard house, this small home was later covered over in brick-patterned shingles. In 1995, it was stuccoed, roofed in metal, and painted beige with light blue trim to create a southwestern flavor, and converted into offices. A chicken coop in back was converted into a guest cottage that opens onto a Spanish-style red flagstone patio.

Photo courtesy of Janis and Bill Keske

The residence has a history of "mixed use." In the 1930s Eva Birdsall ran a rug weaving business here, and in the mid-1940s it was a day nursery.

Washington Avenue Leg (optional)

12

Departing from the residential portion of the tour, this leg takes you to four commercial buildings on Washington Avenue.

908 Washington - Golden Tea Time

This historic home has been converted into a tea room, serving lunch and mid-afternoon tea. This is the half-way point of the tour, and a good place to stop for refreshment!

822 Washington - Coors Credit Union

This modern brick building, constructed in the 1970s and extensively remodeled in 1995, has a schoolhouse feeling. Its two-story massing, gabled entranceway, and wide hipped roof echo the lines of the old North Side School that once stood near Seventh and Washington.

800 Washington - Northgate Building (1996)

This railroad-style building contains business offices and residential suites. It was built on the site of an historic Union Pacific Denver & Gulf Railroad station.

600 Ninth St. - Coors Ceramic Company (1895 - 1990s)

This industrial complex sprawling over two city blocks began as the Golden Pottery Works, operated by John H. Herold on the former site of the local stockyards. Herold's products included "Gem of the Rockies" dishware, tea and chocolate sets, "soap slaps," and ceramic sinks for the School of Mines buildings.

Courtesy Golden Pioneer Museum

Adolph Coors, Jr. took over the business, in part to sustain his company during Prohibition, and in 1915 it employed 37 workers. The ceramic plant was instrumental in defense manufacturing during World War II, and today it produces a variety of ceramic products for industrial and scientific use.

13   900 Arapahoe St.
(circa 1870s)

The two-story clapboard home at 900 Arapahoe Street has a shady front porch. Its wood clapboard exterior was typical of homes on the North Side, as are the ornate paired roof brackets. The shed-roofed portion at the back of the house was possibly a later addition.

Roof brackets and dentils (small squares) like those on the home at 900 Arapahoe were typical in 19th century construction. Carved roof brackets were also used on the wooden, false-front stores originally built in downtown Golden.

14   911 Ninth St.
Spears Residence &
Spears Cash
Grocery
(1920)

William Spears lived in the simple home that adjoined his grocery store. This small brick market was built in the days when few residents owned cars and the neighborhood grocery was a daily stop for local housewives. In the 1940s, Ben Ward ran Ben's Grocery here.

15   921-923 Ninth St.
Baird Residence
(c. 1870)

A petite clapboard duplex, this home has a central bay window flanked by a porch on either side. To the south is a miniature version of this home, possibly built by the same owner.

Eighth Street Leg (optional)

Eighth and Cheyenne Streets, se - Rock Flour Mill Warehouse (c. 1886)

Now called the Stone Mill Building, this is the warehouse remaining from the Rock Flour Mill, one of Golden's three flour mills and possibly the first mill built in the territory.

ROCK FLOUR MILLS

C. H. CASE, Manager.

GOLDEN, - COLO

714 Cheyenne Street (1872) SR

This steep-gabled brick home has a modern addition to accommodate the child care center. Notice how the new addition mirrors the original house in its brick construction and window shapes.

This picture from the May, 1893 "Industrial Edition" of the **Golden Globe** *newspaper shows the Rock Flour Mill and Warehouse. The warehouse still stands today at the southeast corner of Eighth and Cheyenne.*

17 **1013 Ninth St.**   An inviting front porch graces this two-story, painted brick
(c. 1880s)   home. Across the street is where the Golden Paper Mill and a
flour mill were once located; the site is now occupied by three
modern townhouse complexes.

18 **1100 - 1160 Ninth St.**   A row of "gabled-L" vernacular homes, these were possibly
(c. 1900)   speculation homes built by
the same carpenter at the
turn-of-the-century. Notice
and compare how they are
the similar or different
from each other. For example, a shingled dormer was
added to one; another was
stuccoed. Swante
Bergstrom, once secretary
of the Swedish Lutheran Church, lived at 1100 Ninth.

Photo by Susan Goldstein

19 **1145 Ninth St.**

Photo by Susan Goldstein

This tiny gabled
brick home
delights the eye
because of its
small scale, sym-
metry, and its
lathe-turned
porch posts.

20 **1170 Ninth St.**   The Williams Residence is a Classic Cottage - a smaller ver-
Williams Residence   sion of the ubiquitous foursquare. This style was popular in
(1913)   the early 1900s; home owners could purchase a kit for the
entire home for $1,000. The original owner was W. R.
Williams who appears to have been part owner of the
Williams and Cook Cigar Store.

A six-unit row of town houses emulates the neighboring historic homes with wood siding, gabled roofs, and small gabled porches.

1180 - 1190 Ninth St. **21**

The last home on Ninth Street is one of its prettiest — an L-gabled brick home with arched windows complete with flower-carved keystones. A porch nestles in the "El." The house was built for F. K. Palmer who ran Palmer & Sons Vegetable Market in the 1880s.

1200 Ninth St. **22**
Palmer-Hill Residence
(1883)

Photo courtesy of Beth Roark

Lions Park was the contribution of one of Golden's several civic groups in the 1900s, before a local parks and recreation district was organized. The park features a pond, playground, and picnic areas with a fabulous view of Lookout Mountain and Mount Zion. Public restrooms are west of the park.

Lions Park **24**

A bond issue made this $6 million facility possible. Not far from the Golden waterworks where local children once used to skinny-dip in summer and ice-skate in winter, this roomy center offers recreation ranging from swimming to exercise classes to mountain climbing instruction. It also contains drinking fountains, vending machines, and public restrooms. With the building's industrial lines, architects Barker, Rinker, Seacat, & Partners emulated the sloping red roof and beige walls of the now-demolished School of Mines Experimental Plant that stood across Clear Creek.

1470 Tenth St. **25**
Golden Community
Center
1995)

Tip: The tour proceeds south to the creek walk and returns across Clear Creek Bridge to Clear Creek Ranch Park.

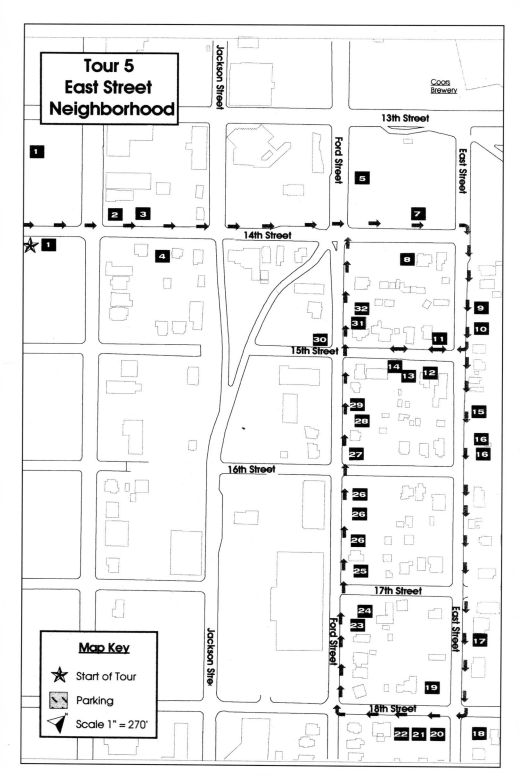

Tour 5
East Street
Neighborhood

Jackson Street

Coors Brewery

13th Street

Ford Street

East Street

5

7

14th Street

1

4

8

32

31

9

10

11

30

15th Street

14

13

12

29

28

15

16

16

27

16th Street

26

26

26

25

17th Street

24

23

17

19

Jackson Street

Ford Street

East Street

Map Key

Start of Tour

Parking

Scale 1" = 270'

18th Street

22 21 20

18

Tour 5

East Golden
Neighborhood

1	Quaintance Building, **NR, LR**
2	1323 Washington Avenue
3	714 Fourteenth Street, **LR**
4	711 Fourteenth, **LR**
5	1200 - 1400 Ford
6	Adolph Coors Brewery
7	View of Castle Rock
8	509 Fourteenth
9	1427 East
10	1501 East
11	500 Fifteenth
12	503 Fifteenth
13	509 Fifteenth
14	515 Fifteenth
15	1515 East
16	1519 and 1521 East
17	1709 East
18	1801 and 1805 East
19	500 Eighteenth
20	501 Eighteenth
21	503 Eighteenth
22	509 Eighteenth
23	1707 Ford
24	1703 Ford
25	1623 Ford
26	1615, 1609, and 1607 Ford
27	1523 Ford
28	1515 Ford
29	1509 Ford
30	1422 Ford
31	1419 Ford
32	1415 Ford

NR = National Register
LR = Local Register

Photo courtesy of Golden Pioneer Museum

***This desperado posing in front of
Castle Rock is actually a geology
student from the School of Mines.***

Tour 5 East Golden Tour

TIME 1 to 1.5 hour **DISTANCE** 1.5 miles

TIPS This tour is a bit hilly, however sidewalks are wheelchair and stroller accessible. Restrooms are available where the tour begins, north of the parking lot at Twelfth and Arapahoe Street.

This tour visits Ford and East Streets, adjacent to downtown Golden. Along both streets are homes dating from the late 1800s and early 1900s. As Golden grew eastward, more modern styles were built. Earlier dwellings are in folk vernacular and Queen Anne styles, followed by Edwardian Vernacular, Dutch Colonial Revival, English/Norman Cottage, and Mission Revival homes. East Golden residents included downtown merchants, brewery workers, School of Mines professors, and employees at the State Industrial School (now the Lookout Mountain School for Boys) located about two miles east of downtown Golden on Old Golden Road.

Photo courtesy of Denver Public Library

Castle Rock dominates east Golden in this early photograph.

Castle Rock is a constant presence on this tour, beginning with the first site — historic headquarters of the Castle Rock Scenic Railway ticket office. As soon as the streetcars reached Golden from Denver in the 1890s, local entrepreneurs offered attractions such as burro rides up Castle Rock, the picturesque basalt rock landmark that rears its head behind the East Golden neighborhood.

At first, tickets were sold from small, wooden shacks near the streetcar depot on Jackson Street. Then local businessman Charles Quaintance built the Castle Rock Scenic Railway to carry visitors to a tea-room, dancehall pavilion, casino, and observatory at the summit of Castle Rock. Quaintance also built a substantial brick storefront at the corner of Thirteenth and Washington, the first site on this tour. Illustrating a traditional Golden entrepreneurial spirit, Quaintance not only sold these tourists a ride up Castle Rock, he also ran a photographed them and offered visitors low-interest real estate loans if they wanted to built a home in the Golden area. The railway operated from 1913 to the early 1920s; the "Castle Rock Resort" burned in 1927.

Burros were not only tourists' transportation, they were also highly photogenic.

The Castle Rock Scenic Railway by night. The searchlight, and lighted railway were probably added to the original photograph.

1 **801 - 805 Thirteenth St.t**
Charles Quaintance Building
(1911)
NR, LR

Charles Quaintance built this storefront trimmed in multi-colored brick to house his investment company, photography studio, and amusement company. From its corner site, Quaintance sold tickets for his Castle Rock Scenic Railway, which carried visitors to the tea-room, dancehall pavilion, casino, and observatory at the summit of Castle Rock. Sightseers from Denver rode the trolley to the depot where Foss Drug now stands, climbing on burros to reach the foot of the funicular railway.

Photo courtesy of Golden Pioneer Museum

In the mid-1920s, the Quaintance building was moved back from its corner site to make way for a gas station. The gas station was later converted into a drive-though bank, and is now a wood-shingled storefront.

The Charles Quaintance Building is visible in the background in this photograph taken during the Armistice Day parade on November 11, 1918. The building was later moved from its corner site its present location on Thirteenth Street.

2 **1323 Washington**
W. A. Rhoads Residence/
Golden Pet Shop
(1903)

The Golden Pet Shop has sold pets to three generations of local children, and the Schloffman family lived in the house behind the store from the 1940s through the present. Herb Schloffman began his pet store in 1947 in the Queen Anne house, building the brick storefront in the 1950s. The original beige brick exterior, lovely shingled gables, arched windows, and stone lintels are visible from the Fourteenth Street side. This house was built in 1903 for a cost of $3,000.

A restaurant now occupies this side-gabled Dutch Colonial Revival house, with the porch enclosed and clad in fishscale shingles. However, a photograph inside shows how the house looked when Mrs. Delaney lived here. Waiters say that her ghost is still here, and claim that windows open by themselves and furniture mysteriously rearranges itself. The reason for these spectral visitations could be that a mortuary was once located here, with embalming done in the basement. Inside, the original woodworking and spindlework gleam darkly, and upstairs offers an incomparable view of Castle Rock.

714 Fourteenth **3**
Delaney Residence
(c. 1910)

This lovely two-story home was converted into a bed and breakfast in 1981. A two-story bay window and thin Italianate windows beautify this vernacular home.

711 Fourteenth St. **4**
Dove Inn Bed and
Breakfast
(c. 1873)

Ford Street **5**

At one time, located along Ford Street between Twelfth and Fourteenth Streets, there were a number of transportation-related enterprises, including livery stables, a saddlery, and a blacksmith shop. The street was named for the Ford Brothers who ran a large gambling tent near Twelfth and Ford in 1859.

Later these blocks became the location of several auto-related businesses, including gas stations and auto repair shops; Ford Street also lay parallel to a street car line running down Jackson Street. Next to downtown, Ford Street is still a transportation hub with a sea of parking lots, a gas station, a drive-through bank, and even a drive-though liquor store.

Photo courtesy of Golden Pioneer Museum

Ford Street in the early 1900s.

Tip: Cross Ford Street on north side of Fourteenth for safety.

6 Adolph Coors Brewery (1873)

The imposing, 3,400-acre concrete-walled plant of Coors Brewery fills the Clear Creek valley, where east Golden farms and orchards once thrived. Today the world's largest single-source brewery, the business was begun in 1873 by one of Golden's many German immigrants — Adolph Coors. The historic Golden City Brewery and Eagle Brewing Company were listed in city directories from the 1800s, but they did not survive. Coors, however, has grown into Golden's major industry, today producing over 20 million barrels of suds per year and visited by 300,000 people annually.

Golden has always been a beer town. Turn-of-the-century beer trains from Golden were enthusiastically met by Denverites. Golden voted against prohibition in 1916, and according to old-timers, stills and bootleggers operated in nearby barn lofts and abandoned farmhouses throughout Prohibition.

Photo courtesy of Colorado School of Mines

This early photo of Coors Brewery shows the original brick buildings with the Coors residence at lower left. In the foreground is the railroad, which played an important role in early Golden and in shipping Coors beer around the state.

First called "Pulpit Rock," this huge basalt monument has
been a landmark of Golden since people first settled here. For

years it appeared as a trade-
mark on every can and bottle of
Coors beer. The scenic railway,
founded by local entrepreneur
Charles Quaintance in the mid
1910s, carried folks up the
north face to the Castle Rock
resort on top. The former railroad grade is still visible from
the north side of Clear Creek.
Plans call for purchasing South
Table Mountain and preserving
it as open space

Photo courtesy of Golden Pioneer Museum

*Tourists loved riding the
Castle Rock Mountain
Railway to the pavilion atop
South Table Mountain.*

One of several Dutch Colonial Revival dwellings in Golden,   **509 Fourteenth St.**   **8**
this house is marked by a bay window and graceful front   (c. 1900)
porch. This style was tremendously popular in the Denver

area in the early 1900s,
with several hundred
designed by architects
Fisher and Fisher.
Because of the gambrel
roof that provided a
roomy second story,
these houses were
regarded as ideal for
newly-married couples
and were nicknamed
"Bride's Delights."

Photo by Susan Goldstein

9 **1427 East St.**
Barb Residence
(1902)

Clark Barb, professor of petroleum engineering at the School of Mines, moved into this bungalow-style home in 1924. The Barb family lived here for several generations, later renting rooms to Mines students.

10 **1501 East St.**
(c. 1890)

The Edwardian/Queen Anne influence on this house is evident in the shingled gable, turned porch posts, and porch spindles.

11 **500 Fifteenth St.**
Quaintance
Residence
(c. 1870s)

This clapboard, gabled "L" was owned by Charles Quaintance, who owned the popular Castle Rock Scenic Railway and Resort. A Golden native, Quaintance graduated from law school and practiced in the town of Cripple Creek before returning to Golden and founding the railway. He later became a local photographer and real estate developer. He also organized the Golden Building and Loan Association and was president of the Chamber of Commerce. Quaintance moved to Denver in 1919 where he became president of Colorado Federal Savings and Loan Association, but he still maintained ownership of several Golden properties.

12 **503 Fifteenth St.**
(c. 1880)

This small well-kept clapboard home has been expanded by a large duplex addition that faces East Street. The traditional elements, such as the gabled roof and wooden shingles, help the new harmonize with the historic.

13 **509 Fifteenth St.**
Youngvall Residence
(1900)

Once owned by Elmer Youngvall this "hipped box" is typical of the early 1900s, with its brick construction, arched windows, and front porch supported by classic columns.

14

515 Fifteenth St.
Petrie Residence
(c. 1890s)

Ira Petrie, owner of Petrie's Pool Hall and Cigar Store on Washington Avenue, resided in this Queen Anne-style home in the mid-1940s.

This Dutch Colonial Revival residence was built by Frederick A. Keener who owned Keener Real Estate and Cattle Company; he was also vice president of the Tramway Corporation and the Standard Building and Loan Association.

1515 East St.
Keener Residence
(1907)

15

1519 and 1521 East St.
(c. 1920)

16

Photo by Susan Goldstein

1519 East Street

Castle Rock frames these two bungalows. This style, popular in the 1930s, is characterized by low-sloping roofs supported by prominent roof brackets, clipped gables, and multi-paned windows. The open-raftered porch on 1519 East is also a typical bungalow feature. An integral garage peers out from the lower story of 1521 East. Both are fronted by a stone retaining wall.

1521 East Street

Photo by Susan Goldstein

This side-gabled woodframe vernacular house was surrounded by land when originally built. A series of additions, including a bathroom and the front porch, were put on over the years.

1709 East Street
Hubert Residence
(c. 1900)

17

18 **1801 and 1805 East St.**

1801 East Street

1805 East Street

These splendid golden-brick homes are Tudor Revival. A curved-gable facade and a battlement parapet extension distinguish 1801 East, while 1805 East is dominated by a prominent chimney and trimmed in dark brown brick. Both have steep roofs, and round-arched windows and doorways characteristic of this style.

19 **500 Eighteenth St.**
Sauter Residence (1893)

This historic sketch of the Sauter residence is from the **Golden Globe.**

Missourian Charles Sauter was a farmer and stockman who purchased a business block on Ford Street. In 1893 the *Golden Globe* called this Queen Anne style home "one of the best houses in the city," featuring eight large rooms, a bathroom, and "all modern conveniences." The Queen Anne style is evident in the asymetrical floor plan, shingled gables, and bay window.

This brick, hip-roofed home with Queen Anne gables was built by Emma R. Wolfe. Charles Albert and Consuelo A.

501 Eighteenth St.
Wolfe Residence
(1903)

20

Ownes lived here from 1935 to 1978. He was a clerk with the Selective Service and she was a stenographer at Colorado School of Mines. Home owners have made several additions over the years.

This diminutive bungalow is distinguished by its prominent stone chimney. The wide overhanging eaves, exposed rafters, and shingle-clad walls

503 Eighteenth St.
Mitchell Residence
(1919)

21

are bungalow elements. In the 1930s and '40s it was the home of Roger Q. Mitchell, superintendent of Golden schools and namesake for Mitchell Elementary School.

A recent owner of this house was Virginia Miller Weigand, writer for the *Colorado Transcript* and *Jefferson County Republican*. Weigand served as chairman of the County Library Board, chairman of the Golden Planning Board, and president of the Golden Chamber of Commerce. Earlier residents included Gary C. Kerr, who was active in the Republican party and served as sheriff and police chief. This was previously the home of James and Gertrude Miller; Gertrude was president of the Golden Library and James was editor of the *Transcript* and founded the Republican.

509 Eighteenth St.
Kerr/Miller/Weigand Residence
(c. 1900)

22

Dominated by two towering blue spruces, the house has been significantly remodeled. It retains an entryway with three round arches.

23 **1707 Ford St.**
Koenig Residence
(c. 1878)

Rudolph Koenig emigrated from Switzerland and ran a Golden brick plant with his brother. He was later involved with the Golden Smelting Works. This historic house was updated in the 1920s with Craftsman-style shingled walls, stuccoed and timbered gable ends, and multi-paned windows.

24 **1703 Ford St.**
Dorothy Foss
O'Byrne Residence
(1905)

Dorothy, the widow of Henry Foss, lived here while married to Joe O'Byrne, a geometry professor at the Colorado School of Mines. Dorothy managed the Foss Drug store until the late 1930s when her son Frederick Allen "Heine" Foss took it over. For a few years Heine and his wife lived here in the basement. The Mission Style home has a curvilinear roof parapet, widely overhanging eaves, classical porch columns, and leaded glass windows. Note the stone lintels and sills.

Photo by Susan Goldstein

25 **1623 Ford St.**
Woodbridge
Residence
(1910)

This Edwardian Vernacular home is characterized by a front-gabled roof, gable-end shingles, flared eaves, arched windows with sills, and an inset porch. Historic owners included Samuel Ellis, Herman and Emma Kathman, and Edward C. Furniss, who ran a Washington Avenue blacksmith shop.

Although dramatically altered by additions, stucco, or wide modern siding, these three historic homes possess a traditional L-gable pattern resembling those in the introduction for this tour.

1615, 1609, and 1607 Ford St.
(c. 1870s)

26

The homes closer to downtown Golden are Ford Street's oldest. Many residents ran local businesses, worked at Coors, or taught at the School of Mines. Charles S. Staples was a merchant tailor and Golden's justice of the peace.

1523 Ford St.
Staples Residence
(1889)

27

A 1905 "Pretty Homes" edition of the *Colorado Transcript* reported that Staples' lovely Queen Anne had a spacious basement, three commodious living rooms, a large hall, and "plenty of closets and pantry, etc., for convenience in housekeeping." Its shingled gables, full-front porch with spindlework trim and decorative brackets are Queen Anne-style details. The arched windows with fleur-de-lis and leaf pattern are similar to those seen in the Twelfth Street neighborhood.

This English/Norman Cottage with its brown brick trim and round-arched doorway is a contemporary of those at the corner of Eighteenth and East Streets and others near the School of Mines.

1515 Ford Street
Beckner Residence
(1938)

28

Although somewhat altered, this represents Golden's early housing stock. Alex Jameson, an early owner of the house, was Deputy County Clerk of Jefferson County, and was involved in selling real estate and insurance. He was also a prominent Golden lawyer and school district director. He later became a probate judge and presided over the marriage of Louise Weber to Adolph Coors.

1509 Ford Street
Jameson Residence
(1884)

29

30 **1422 Ford Street**
Davidson Residence
(c. 1878)

The original owner of this brick home was John C. Davidson, a licensed embalmer. He ran a furniture and undertaker

goods store on Washington Avenue that he later sold to the owner of Woods Mortuary. The house is distinguished by its steep gabled roof, and tall, narrow windows with thick pedimented (triangular) stone lintels.

31 **1419 Ford Street**
Williams Residence
(1893)

Mary Dillon and Mary C. Williams were early owners of this cross-gabled vernacular home. The ornamental shingles and decorative woodworking on the porch are elements of the Queen Anne style.

32 **1415 Ford Street**
Matthews Residence
(c. 1873)

This brick dwelling features a front-gabled roof and full front porch supported by classical wooden columns. This was the longtime home of James J. Matthews, a Golden cattleman.

> **Tip:** Cross Ford Street on north side of Fourteenth for safety and return to the parking lot at Twelfth and Arapahoe (see the map).

Sites Worth Further Investigation

The Golden Chamber of Commerce has information on these sites.

Clear Creek Ranch Park- **Tour 1**

Astor House Hotel Museum - **Tour 2**

Rocky Mountain Quilt Museum - **Tour 2**

CSM Geology Museum - **Tour 3**

Foothills Art Center - **Tour 3**

Golden DAR Museum - **Tour 4**

Coors Brewery - **Tour 5**

Colorado Railroad Museum

New Jefferson County Courthouse

Camp George West

Magic Mountain/Apex/Heritage Mountain

Dinosaur Ridge

Red Rocks Amphitheater

Jefferson County Nature Center

Boettcher Mansion

Lookout Mountain and the Lariat Trail

Buffalo Bill Museum

Mother Cabrini Shrine

Preserving Golden's Architecture - How it Works

Historic preservation is no accident. There are several elements that contribute to maintaining the integrity of Golden's historic architecture.

Historic Preservation Ordinance

An ordinance passed in 1983 established a process for designating local landmarks and establishing a board appointed by City Council to oversee preservation of those homes and buildings. The round local landmark plaques mark these sites as being significant to local history or architecturally outstanding.

Historic Preservation Board

This seven-person board implements Golden's historic preservation ordinance. The HPB works in conjunction with the Golden Planning Department and the Golden building inspector.

The board meets monthly to:

1   Evaluate local historical site and district designations, forwarding recommendations to City Council.

2   Provide advice and guidance regarding alterations to designated historic sites or districts.

3   Review plans for proposed work on designated historic homes and buildings.

4   Oversee a comprehensive inventory of Golden's historic structures and districts.

5   Evaluate and comment on decisions by public agencies concerning physical development and land use patterns affecting historic sites and districts.

State Register of Historic Properties and National Register of Historic Places

These two lists of significant buildings, structures, objects, districts, and historic archaeological sites are coordinated through the Office of Archaeology and Historic Preservation at the Colorado Historical Society in Denver. Advantages of listing include:

1   Formal recognition of a property's importance to national, state, or local history.

2   Eligibility to compete for grants from Colorado's State Historical Fund.

3   Eligibility to apply for state tax credits for restoration, rehabilitation, or preservation of properties.

Listing in the State or National Register imposes no restriction on what a private property owner may do with their property. It does not impose any responsibilities upon the owner for maintenance or restoration. For information on historic preservation in Golden, call the Planning Department **(303) 384-8097**.

Glossary

ashlar
Hewn stone blocks with even faces and square edges and laid in horizontal courses with vertical joints, as opposed to unhewn stone straight from the quarry.

bargeboard
Projecting boards placed against the incline of the gable of a building and hiding the ends of the horizontal roof timbers; sometimes decorated.

battered
Referring to a porch post whose base is broader, tapering to a more narrow top. Often associated with the Arts and Crafts style.

bay window
Projecting, often three-sided window. Often seen with Italianate and Queen Anne-style homes.

board and batten siding
A siding consisting of vertical application of boards trimmed by thin wood strips.

Arts and Crafts style
A front-gabled home with low-slanting roof and similarly-roofed porch. May also have projecting eaves, battered porch columns, and open-gabled porch. Often combing brick, wood or stone, this style was prominent between 1910 and 1925. The one-story version is called a bungalow.

baluster/balustrade
Small, bulging, vase-shaped column. A series of these is called a balustrade and may form a porch railing.

bracket, knee-bracket
A supporting piece, often L-shaped, projecting from a wall to support a roof, cornice, or other item.

bungalow style
A front-gabled home with low-slanting roof and similarly-roofed porch. The bungalow generally features projecting eaves, battered porch columns, and open-gabled porch, and brick, wood, or stone building material. This style was prominent style between 1910 and 1925; the two-story version is considered Arts and Crafts style.

clapboard
A long thin board, thicker on one edge than the other, used in covering the outer walls of buildings; of or made of clapboard. Describe as either narrow or wide. Wide is often more recent and may be vinyl or aluminum.

classic column
A column with pronounced capital (top) and a base (bottom).

cobblestone
A naturally rounded stone, larger than a pebble and smaller than a boulder, formerly used in paving.

Glossary (cont.)

corbel, corbeling
Stepped arrangements of stones or bricks, with each course projecting beyond the one below. Used at rooflines of flat-roofed buildings, especially commercial buildings for structural reinforcement.

course
Row of laid brick or stone.

cornice
Any prominent, projecting molded feature surmounting a wall, doorway, or other construction. Most often seen on commercial buildings.

cross gable
Multiple gables facing both front and sides.

curvilinear parapets
A low wall used at edge of a roof, distinguished by a round curve in the center. This element is often associated with Mission Style popular in the early 1900s.

dentils
A series of closely-spaced small rectangular blocks used at the cornice, especially in classical architecture. Often seen in brick Italianate commercial architecture.

dormer window
A small gabled or shed-roofed window projecting from a roof.

double-hung window
A window having two vertical sashes, each closing a different part of the opening.

facade
The front of a building, especially an imposing or decorative one. Most often used in reference to commercial buildings.

fishscale shingling
Often seen in gable end, round-ended shingles.

foursquare
A boxy, two-story house style popular in the early 1900s, featuring a hipped roof, one or more dormer windows, and a front porch.

frieze
A decorative, often carved, band near the top of a wall; most often seen in commercial architecture.

Edwardian Vernacular style
A post-Victorian style resembling Queen Anne but with fewer decorative details. Elements include gabled roofs, gable-end shingling, and a front porch.

front gabled
Having gable(s) facing front of the property, toward the street.

Glossary (cont.)

gabled roof
A roof with two sloping sides that meet at the top, forming a triangular shape. The triangular portion is called the "gable."

gambrel roof
A four-sided gable, often associated with American barn. The gambrel roof was a characteristic of Dutch Colonial Revival. The house layout may be front-, side-, or cross-gabled.

Gothic Revival
An architectural style popular in the mid-1800s, characterized by two-story height, a steeply gabled roof, elaborate window tops, and wood trim along the roof gable.

half-timbering
Linear, decorative woodworking applied over stucco to imitate English half-timbering, which consisted of wooden structural supports filled in.

hipped roof
Pyramid-shaped roof, generally seen on foursquare or Italianate style houses.

Italianate style
An architectural style popular in the mid-1800s. Typically, a two-story, square-shaped or L-shaped house with a widely overhanging hipped roof supported by decorative roof brackets. This style is marked by tall, thin windows, symmetrically placed and often arched. The Italianate home usually no porch.

keystone
Stone inserted in apex (top) of an arch.

lap siding
Siding composed of overlapping, horizontal strips, which may be wood, vinyl, or aluminum. Wood version is also called "clapboard."

lintel
The horizontal architectural member supporting the weight above an opening such as a window or a door.

Mission style
This style is distinguished by a curvilinear shaped gable. There is often a small round or quatrefoil window or ornament. Typical building materials are stucco exterior with clay tile roof.

parapet
Low wall used at edge of a roof.

pilaster
A shallow pier or rectangular column, projecting only slightly from a wall.

Glossary (cont.)

Queen Anne style
An asymmetrical house style marked by multiple gables and two-story, often brick, construction. Features include shingles in gable end, sunburst in gable, bay windows, decorative woodworking, turrets, and multi-paned windows.

shingle
A thin piece of wood, slat, metal, or asbestos laid in overlapping rows to cover the roofs and walls of buildings. Notable when wood shingling appears in the gable end of a house or on the exterior walls. Shapes of shingles include fishscale (rounded) and variegated.

side-gabled
Gable(s) perpendicular to street front, so that house is parallel to street.

siding
Sheathing placed over exterior walls. Aluminum and vinyl siding are wider and shinier than historic wooden siding. Siding materials from the 1940s included asphalt and asbestos.

spindlework
Woodworking such as railings or balustrades, composed of short, turned or circular ornaments that resemble spindles.

stucco
An exterior finish for masonry or frame walls usually composed of cement, sand and hydrated lime mixed with water and laid on wet. Often considered to degrade a building's historical integrity.

transom window
Window panel above a door or window.

Tudor Revival style
A style popular in the late teens and early twenties, this style employs beige brick with a steeply sloping roof, a dominant exterior chimney, and often an arched doorway.

turned porch posts
Rounded, shaped posts made by turning on a lathe.

vernacular style
A common style, constructed by local craftsman or home owner. Building materials were typically brick or wood. These ordinary houses were had varied floorplans and orientation, including front-gabled, side-gabled, gabled-L, or cross-gabled.

Bibliography

_____. *Colorado Business Directories*. 1890, 1900, 1910.

_____. *Golden Globe Industrial Edition,* May 19, 1893.

_____. *Golden Transcript*. "Pretty Homes" issue. Dec. 28, 1905.

_____. *Rocky Mountain Directory & Gazeteer for 1871*. Denver: S. S. Wallihan & Co. 1870.

Abbott, Dan. *Twelfth Street Historic District - Survey Update*. Golden: City of Golden Planning Department. 1992.

Berthoud, E. L. "History of Jefferson County." *History of Clear Creek and Boulder Valley*. Chicago: O. L. Baskin & Co. 1880.

Budd, Montgomery R. Jr., "Colorado and its School of Mines." *The Colorado School of Mines Magazine*. Golden: Colorado School of Mines. Jan. 1930 - July 1930.

Brown, Georgina. *The Shining Mountains*. Gunnison: B&B Printers. 1976.

Fanning, Mary. *For the Golden Times*. Golden: Golden Chamber of Commerce. 1977.

Golden Historic Preservation Board. *1996 Resource Guide to Historic Preservation in Golden*. Golden: City Planning Department. 1996.

Hoyt, Mary E. "A Short History of the Colorado School of Mines." *The Mines Magazine*. Golden: Colorado School of Mines. June, 1949.

Kimball, George M. *Illustrated Golden and Vicinity*. Golden: Kimball and Slingerland. 1902.

Morgan, Jesse R. *A World School*. Denver: Sage Books. 1955.

Noel, Dr. Thomas J. *Buildings of the United States: Colorado Volume*. Oxford: Oxford University Press. 1997.

Ryland, Charles. "Golden - History of the Chrysopolis." *The 1960 Brand Book*. Denver: Denver Westerners. 1960.

Scheunemann, Toni L. The Foothills Art Center: *The Crowning Glory of Golden's Courthouse Hill*. Golden: Foothills Art Center. 1981.

Simmons, R. Laurie, Thomas Simmons, and Christine Whitacre. *Historic Building Surveys*. Golden: City Planning Department. 1988, 1989, 1990, and 1991.

Wagenbach, Loraine, editor. *A Woman's Life in Golden (1902 - 1980)*. Golden: Pioneer Delphian Study Club. 1980.

Wagenbach, Lorraine and Jo Ann Thistlewood. *Golden in the 19th Century*. Littleton: Harbinger House. 1987.

Golden's Twelfth Street Historic District